North Berwick - Wish You Were Here!

200 Years of 'Summertime' in the Royal Burgh of North Berwick

John Fergie

First Published in 2013 by
Bramble Publishing
Bramble Cottage
Dirleton
East Lothian
EH39 5EH

www.bramblepublishing.co.uk

ISBN 978-0-9574562-2-8

Printed in Scotland by Allander Print Ltd.
www.allander.com

Acknowledgements

The author would like to thank the following for their assistance during his research without whom this book would not have been possible :-

Ian Archibald, Stewart Auld, Vanda Baillie, Sheila Baird, Ritchie Bathgate, Tom Bathgate, Emma Bell, Allister Blair, Jean Boal, Derek Braid, Tom Brock, George Brown, Margaret Burgon, Harvey Butterworth, Ronnie Coates-Walker, Raymond Coventry, Anne Cowan, Mike Cowan, Ada Craig, Jean Crawford, Lyle Crawford, Dino Cuchi, Rosemary Cunningham, Tommy Dale, Jimmy Dalgleish, Lynn Dalgleish, Sir Hew Hamilton Dalrymple, George Denholm, Margaret Dinning, John Edwards, Gordon Elliot, Douglas Ferguson, Tom Fergusson, Betty Gilford, Ian Goodall, Ian Gordon, Len Groom, Peter Hammond, Sir Peter Heatly, Hugh Henderson, Jim Hill, Ted Hill, Rosey Holliday, Alex Hutchison, Ina Hutchison, Allan and Jean Hutchison, Jim Hutchison, Anne Hutton, Sandy Jenner, Sheila Kennedy, Frances Laing, Joan Lemmon, Stroma Lennox, Norma Louden, Colin Lourie, Laurie Lumsden, Pat MacAuley, Donald McCulloch, Rosie McCulloch, Alec McDonald, Shona McDonald, Oliver McKemmie, Jane McMinn, Bill Macnair, Peggy McNicoll, Tom Main, Hermione Malcolm, Chris Marr, John Masterton, Bob Miller, Cherie Miller, Barbara Montgomery, Bee Moskal, Helen Murray, Wendy Neill, Rosie Oberlander, Len Patey, Benji Pearson, Betty Porteous, Elma Ritchie, Walter Scott, Douglas Seaton, Jimmy Shand Jnr., John Shaw, Jeanette Simpson, George Skirving, Alec Smart, Eric Smith, Katheryn Smith, Margaret Smith, Chris Spencer, John Starr, Craig Statham, Sandy Steel, Alistair and Irene Stewart, Jim Stewart, Stirling Stewart, Gail Storey, Bryan Thomson, Doreen Thomson, Elsie Thorburn, Rev. David Torrence, Betty Treharne, David Turner, Ella Vlandy, Eric Wales, Catherine Watt, John Wightman, Marjory Wilson, Martin Wilson, Ross Wilson, Gwen Wright.

East Lothian Council Museum and Library Departments, East Lothian Yacht Club, Evan's Trust, Fringe by the Sea, North Berwick Bowling Club, North Berwick Golf Club, North Berwick Highland Games, North Berwick In Bloom, Scottish Seabird Centre, Warrender Baths Club.

Thanks also to Christine Gollan for all her help, support and advice.

Contents

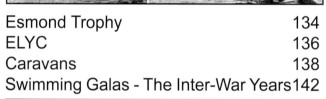

Introduction

Lying at the mouth of the Firth of Forth, on its southern shore, North Berwick - at the start of the nineteenth century - was a small sleepy fishing village. The parish was populated by barely 1500 residents with just over half living within the Burgh itself and the size of the town had probably changed little over the preceding hundred years. An 1832 map shows the town, extending in today's terms from the North Berwick Clubhouse in the west to Quality Street in the east and consisting mainly of the High Street, West Gate, Market Place and Quality Street. Little today remains of the buildings which existed then – only one or two of the High Street shops and possibly a couple of the fishing cottages in Forth Street, formerly Back Street.

Agriculture provided the main employment in the parish, with the fishing industry, albeit to a more limited extent, being the largest provider of employment for townsfolk. Shopkeepers would ply their trade from one, or at most, one and a half storey properties on the High Street with occasional travellers passing through selling their wares. A regular market was held at the south end of Quality Street where it meets the High Street.

Occasional well-to-do visitors might appear in the summer months. Arriving in a horse-drawn carriage or sailing vessel, they might have visited the local antiquities, perhaps promenade along the links taking in the sea air or perhaps sea-bathing in the bracing waters of the Forth - the new fashionable pastime in those Regency days. They may have

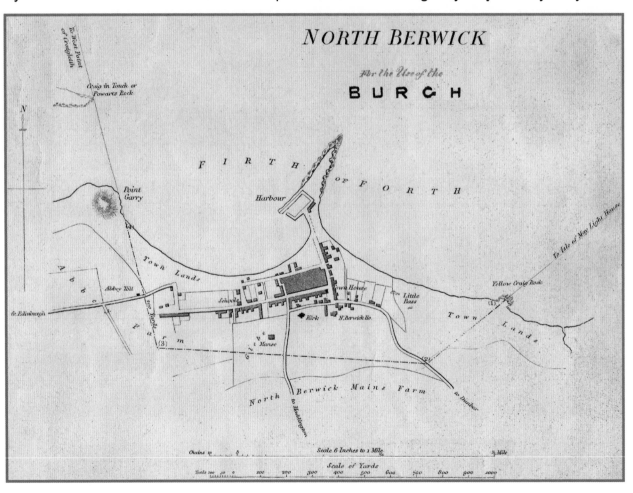

Extent of the Burgh of North Berwick 1832

6

North Berwick c1845

stayed with a relative or friend in the tree-lined Quality Street, or even at an inn, enjoying the quaint banter of the locals. If they were very well-to-do they may have stayed with the local gentry in their country house and those acquainted with the Dalrymple family may even have been invited to join a shooting party to the Bass Rock. North Berwick must have seemed very quaint to the gentlefolk from the metropolitan areas. A town stuck in time - probably similar to many other rural towns at the time.

There were stirrings of change though. North Berwick was slowly being recognised by a wider audience as a place to visit. In 1824 *The Scotsman* reported that in April of that year a spring fair of exhibitions and amusements was held – including horse, swine and ass races, cock-fighting and various foot-races. Of particular note was a sack race where 'eight men (smiths, tailors, etc) were tied in sacks and had to run a certain distance thus fettered, and, by their tumbling and awkward gambols, afforded much sport. Nearly five thousand people attended, among whom were observed; his Grace the Duc of Guige, Peer of France, and his Duchess; the Hon. Lord Elcho; Major-General Dalrymple and Lady; Captains Brown, Cheyne, and

Baird, and a full assemblage of the most respectable farmers and others, from a great distance. A great number of the gentlemen who had exerted themselves in getting up the sports dined together in Blair's Inn, and spent the evening with much hilarity.'

The town's growing popularity as a place to be seen in is recorded in the Statistical Account of 1839 when the author for the Parish of North Berwick, The Rev. Robert Balfour Graham, records that 'the geniality of summer and autumn is amply attested to in the crowded influx of strangers for the enjoyment of sea-bathing and the perambulation among the beautiful scenery around.'

Soon, events were about to happen that would change North Berwick forever to create the town that is known all over the world, the town we know and love today.

First to make its impact was golf. At that time a game exclusive to the aristocracy and their like, it was spreading its wings and migrating down the Forth coast. Although the game had been played in the town for over two hundred years it was only in 1832 that the North Berwick Club was founded. After a bracing round on the Links the members would sup and dine in a marquee pitched by the first tee – reputed to be in the vicinity of what became known as Elcho Green.

Secondly, during the second quarter of the eighteenth century, parcels of land were put up for feuing - thereby allowing building stances for villas to be sold. Then in the late 1840s a spur-line was built from the main Edinburgh-London line at Drem to the Royal Burgh which was finally opened in 1850 ensuring its accessibility.

North Berwick, the backwater, was about to emerge from its chrysalis into a fine Victorian spa town stretching along its shore with the building of fine villas along the East Bay and West Links, and with many of its ramshackle older buildings demolished and replaced by houses and shops more fitting to the period.

NORTH-BERWICK.

GROUND FOR VILLAS.

THE Magistrates and Town Council of North Berwick, having obtained from Mr Swinton, Architect, Haddington, a Plan for feuing out into VILLAS, the small field lying in the North East part of the Royalty, are ready to enter into terms for the same. It is proposed to divide the field into six stances, alloting to each stance sufficient ground for a well sized Garden and the usual appendages.

The situation is peculiarly adapted for the purpose of feuing, as it commands one of the finest and most romantic sea views on the coast, embracing at once the opposite coast of Fife, Isle of May, the Bass, and adjoining Islands; and the beach, to which it is quite close, is well known to possess superior advantages for bathing. So great indeed has been the attraction to North Berwick of late years, in this respect, that the demand for houses has much exceeded the accommodation at present available for sea bathing quarters.

To Builders a more eligible opening could not be presented, or one which is more likely to yield a handsome return on their outlay. Its distance from Edinburgh, only 23 miles, and to which there is such ready access by means of Coaches going and returning every day—its unrivalled beach—the increasing influx of strangers during Summer; and the agreeable walks in its vicinity, all combine to render North Berwick one of the most desirable situations to be met with for the erection of Marine Villas, even to a much greater extent than what is now contemplated.

The Magistrates will give every encouragement to intending Feuars. The Plans will be seen in the hands of Mr Hislop, the Town Treasurer.

Applications may be made to Mr Hislop, or to Messrs Fraser & Crawford, W.S. 29, Elder Street, Edinburgh.

North Berwick, 3rd May 1843.

Advert from April 1843 for plots of land now know as Marine Parade.

By the 1860s this pretty resort had become the place to be seen, particularly among those who could afford first class accommodation. In 1861 the *Haddingtonshire Courier* started to print a weekly list of hotel and letting accommodation with the names of their respective resident visitors, along with other useful information for the visitor – high water times; train departure and arrival times; the uplift time for post; and the colours of funnels (representing the owners of steamers) passing up or down the Forth. This popularity and desire to stay in North Berwick was summed up in the summer of 1868 when the *'Haddingtonshire Courier'* reported: 'the tropical state of the temperature in the country has induced a general desire for the cooling air of the seaside, and numerous applications, which unfortunately could not be responded to, have been received from London and elsewhere for lodgings of a superior character. These are all taken up at present and are likely to be so till the end of the season.'

Accommodation needs had become so acute with demand outstripping supply, that the rush was on to build more quality hotels and accommodation. The Royal Hotel, completed in 1861 with 14 elegant and spacious suites, was the first purpose-built hotel of any size to be built in the town. Demand was so strong to stay there that over the next few years, two additions were made to the property providing a further 45 rooms. Over the years the town's portfolio of hotel accommodation continued to increase most notably with the building of the Marine Hotel in 1875 and Tantallon Hall in 1908.

Steamers were first reported as visiting the waters off North Berwick as early as the 1830s although it was some years later before they allowed passengers to disembark for a brief visit to the town. In the summer of 1860 the steamer 'Star' made a number of excursions to North Berwick allowing its passengers a short break in the town, and in 1866 the firm of Steadman, Harrison & Dykes started running regular trips between Leith and North Berwick with their tug 'Powerful', picking up passengers en-route to the Isle of May. The town soon became a favourite stopping place with other steamship companies

from Leith, Aberdour and Elie - all of which started landing visitors regularly. Some visitors were happy with a walk along the beach but for others, eager to show off the latest bathing fashions, there was a quick dip in the briny. In July 1869 the *'Courier'* reported that at North Berwick 'continental fashions had to some extent been introduced by

Royal Hotel Advert from c1873

some of the fair votaries of Neptune with more than one of the lady bathers taking her ablutions in the prettiest of costumes comprising scarlet tunic, knickerbockers, and light coloured boots – the *tout ensemble* being of the most charming character and likely to be very generally adopted.' Others visitors, reported by the same publication in August 1874, were more daring 'paying their respects to Father Neptune by aquatic performances in *puris naturalibus*,' though it also reported that the antics were more 'energetic than graceful.'

The last quarter of the eighteenth century saw a steady increase in day-trippers to North Berwick. A common sight at the station were the special trains laid on to bring influxes of factory and office workers. Trains would arrive from all over central Scotland almost daily throughout the season, bringing hoards of workers many of whom would be visiting the seaside for the first time. As we can imagine the streets and links were at times, during the season, very busy: crowded and lively with visiting workers enjoying, in most cases, their only days holiday of the year. Happily there were few reports of trouble.

During the second half of the eighteenth century the High Street and West Gate were almost completely rebuilt with fashionable tenement buildings and the road laid with causeway stones, which then attracted purveyors of quality food produce and warehousemen who could supply the finest continental goods. Many retailers offered a house agent service too, no doubt keen to establish strong relationships with the households - mainly through the butler. Butchers, bakers, fishmongers and grocers were well represented in the town. In addition a number of Edinburgh retailers followed their clientele down to North Berwick, opening shops in their customers' resort of choice – R&T Gibson, Methven & Simpson, and Johnston Green to mention but a few.

In 1870 George Ferrier, a family grocer and wine merchant, started publishing a guide to the town and its environs - 'North Berwick: Queen of Watering Places', complete with a summary of the rules of golf and instructions in the art of sea-bathing – including when to bathe; the condition of the bather; how long a bather ought to remain in the water and why there must be no hesitation on the part of the bather. His well-received guide proclaimed North Berwick to be the most picturesque of watering places excelling all, including the best bathing-places in Europe and even comparable with Biarritz – perhaps the source of 'Biarritz of the North', a term so frequently used to describe North Berwick.

During the middle and late nineteenth century many jobs were lost with the demise of the local fishing industry to be replaced by occupations such as cab-drivers, grooms, letter carrier, gardeners, porters, carters, green-keepers and caddies as well as numerous other positions created by shopkeepers, hoteliers

OLD AND NEW NORTH BERWICK CENTRE OF HIGH STREET.

Sketch of North Berwick High Street c1872
The older tenements on the left were demolished and replaced with the Police Station and the tenements on the right are the same as those today albeit with different shop fronts and occupants. In 1872 the shop on the extreme right was occupied by George Ferrier, grocer and wine merchant.

and building firms. Many of those contracted in the building of the new villas continued afterwards to provide repair and maintenance work and some established their own businesses.

Building work continued unabated at the start of the new century with further development to the west and south of the town. However the most important change was the building and opening of a new swimming pond, at the Platcock Rocks, at a cost of £527 - almost all of which was raised by public subscription and local fundraising events. The opening ceremony in September 1900 was conducted by the Right Hon. Lord Justice-General in front of a paying audience of nearly three thousand. The pond became the diamond in North Berwick's summer crown for almost a century. A few years later the adjoining esplanade, newly surfaced with concrete, became the summer home to travelling entertainers who enthralled spectators with lively entertainment.

In 1900 North Berwick could offer visitors quality accommodation, a choice of quality shops supplying the best produce, fresh sea air, and ease of access, and to all some of the best golfing in the world. North Berwick was the fashionable place to be seen during the Edwardian era and continued to be so through to the sixties, the only exceptions being during both World Wars.

Visitors and excursionists to the Royal Burgh could look forward to seasonal enjoyment throughout the whole season – putting competitions, yachting regattas, tennis tournaments, rowing cobles, swimming galas, fancy dress galas, midnight bathing, golf on the links, trips to the islands of the Forth, Church of Scotland Seaside Mission, lifeboat galas, sandcastle and model yacht competitions and all forms of live entertainment.

Following a dip in popularity during the latter half of the twentieth century, particularly after the introduction of cheap package holidays to continental Europe, North Berwick, in the twenty-first century, has once again become a popular destination with both day-trippers and those wishing to stay longer. Once again the town can offer excellent accommodation and a choice of eateries: year round golf; wonderful walking and cycling and visitor attractions; and during the season a varied mix of entertainments including the increasingly popular 'Fringe by the Sea.'

Dalrymple Hotel, Quality Street c1890
The position of carriage driver and chamber maid (lady in white pinifore) were probably dependant on the influx of summer visitors and therefore seasonal. In the distance some men hang around a doorway to the property known as 'Brodie's Stables' - possibly taking a break from mucking out or awaiting customers to hire their horses and carriages for the day. The landau and driver, patiently waiting on the cobbled street, may await a guest from the Dalrymple Arms for a drive around the more popular visitor sites. This would cost about £1, well beyond the reach of humbler visitors and certainly not within the means of most locals.

Canty Bay

For over two hundred years visitors to North Berwick have been taking trips to Canty Bay. Lying about two miles east of North Berwick, Canty Bay, a small hamlet on the shore of a semi-circular bay was once regarded as the port for the Bass Rock, which lies opposite. The policies once included a small single storey inn, cottages, stables and offices as well as about two acres of land, all let by the Dalrymple family. Also included were the grazing rights on the Bass Rock and the 'taking' of solan geese - all for an annual rent of about £30 with the tenant also expected to provide transport to the island.

In the early part of the nineteenth century, the Kelly family were tenants. As well as income from the sale of the much prized 'Bass' mutton they would earn monies derived from the sale of solan geese, gannets, which at the time were much prized for their flesh, oil, eggs and feathers. In Spring a climber would clamber over the precipitous cliff tops of the Bass to push young gannets into the sea below, to be picked up by men in a boat. The annual income from this source was in excess of £100 with Kelly taking all reasonable steps to protect the business, particularly from passengers shooting from visiting steamers.

With the coming of the railway to North Berwick in 1850, Canty Bay and the Bass became even more popular as destinations for visitors including antiquarians eager to explore the ruins at Tantallon and Auldhame. A popular walking route was down through the Lady's Walk and along the clifftops, maybe stopping for refreshment at Kelly's hostelry, before continuing their hike to take in the impressive clifftop ruins. The final half-mile walk along the ridge afforded the magnificent vista of Sligo's mansion at Seacliff.

BASS ROCK

WHEREAS, during the last Season, many of the Solan Geese on and about the Bass Rock, were shot and otherwise wickedly destroyed by persons in Steam-Vessels, and other Vessels passing and making trips to the Island, and also by persons in small Boats from North Berwick and other places adjacent,

NOTICE IS HEREBY GIVEN,

That any person or persons who may hereafter be found Shooting at or otherwise Destroying or Disturbing the Solan Geese on or about the Bass Island, will be Prosecuted according to Law; and Captains and Masters of Steam-Boats and others, are requested to take Notice, that they will be held responsible for persons on board their respective Vessels who may be guity of such conduct.

Persons giving information against Offenders to JAMES KELLY, the Tenant, at Canty Bay, or William Lockhart, at Wamphray, the Overseer on the North Berwick Estate, will be suitably rewarded.

16th April 1836

Above Left: A romantic sketch of Canty Bay and the Bass Rock c1830
Bottom Left : Kelly's warning to poachers of Solan Geese. 1836

For early Victorian antiquarians who were happy to walk to their destination, possibly through the beautifully kept Lady's Walk (top left) before heading eastwards along the clifftops, their journey would allow them to observe the natural coastal beauty before glimpsing their goal, Tantallon (top right), before walking onwards to the ruins of Auldhame (below right) which overlook The Gegan with its delightful little harbour, and finally Sligo's mansion which while in the ownership of his successor, Andrew Laidlay, was destroyed in a fire on the night of July 28th 1907.

A Victorian shooting party on Bass Rock. c1875

HADDINGTONSHIRE
BASS ROCK
AND
CANTY BAY HOTEL

ENTRY WHITSUNDAY 1891

CANTY BAY HOTEL, about two miles from North Berwick, with stable, &c., offices, four cottages, and two acres of land. Additional land might be ultimately be had if required. Sole privilege to land visitors on Bass Rock, and right to grazing and rabbits thereon.

The tenant will require to have a good steam launch and other boats.

Further particulars apply to -
J & F Anderson, W.S.,
48 Castle Street, Edinburgh.

Above : The old inn at Canty Bay popular with shooting parties c1878
Inset : George Adams' advert for Solan Geese eggs - 'highly appreciated at the Royal Table'. c1856

Advert from 'The Scotsman' 24 January 1891.

By the summer season of 1860 John Blair, a merchant on the High Street, was offering omnibuses to Canty Bay and Tantallon for the modest fare of one shilling. Visits to the Bass by the members of Royal family included Prince Albert in July 1864 who, as a guest of Sir Hew Dalrymple, was rowed over to the island by George Adams, the tenant at the time. The party climbed to the top of the island, bagging a few gannets on their ascent. Adams had a reputation for serving up the flesh of Solan Geese in place of beef steak, only to tell the guest after their meal.

Accommodation for the tenant was in the form of the small inn close to the shore. In about 1882, the original building was enlarged with the addition of a second storey, opening as a new marine hotel by the then-tenant C. J. Downie. It is possible that it was Downie who introduced the steam launch as a means of conveying parties over to the Bass. His vessel named "Spark" was 25 feet in length and fitted with 'Cormack's' Patent Surface Condensing Engines and 'Field' Tube Boiler. When there was inclement weather Downie would calm passenger nerves by telling them that "Spark" had earned an A1 character by having gone on such distant voyages as Anstruther, and even Leith, in very boisterous weather, and that it had behaved well! Downie also provided tented accommodation in the form of a marquee with tables and forms for 70 people in which he served luncheons, teas and all other refreshments.

North Berwick general practioner Dr Crombie with family and friends on a trip to the Bass Rock c1890
Among those present - From left, Miss (or Mrs) Gillies Smith (lady with hat with flowers), ? , ? , Mr D B Swan (bowler hat and black moustache), Mrs Swan, Mrs Robert Lyle,
Frank (later Dr) Crombie, Mrs Crombie, Dr Crombie, Miss Frances L Crombie, Mrs Lyle, Lady Dalrymple, Miss Gillies Smith, Mr A Gillies Smith, Provost Peter Brodie, ? , ? , ? ,
? , John R Whitecross (white top hat and beard). In Front : Miss Dalrymple and Jock Dalrymple.

Downie who was very well-informed on the history of the Bass and its birdlife often invited the school children at Halflandbarns for a trip to the island - happily sharing his knowledge with the young pupils, and afterwards treating the children to buns and lemonade which were followed with games and prizes.

In 1891 the Dalrymple Estate was looking for a new tenant for Canty Bay, to replace Downie's successor of a few years, Finlay C. Manson. The position, as advertised, gave the tenant grazing rights and rabbits on the island but there was no mention of shooting gannets! By this time the demand for the solan goose had almost evaporated.

However demand to visit the island was still as popular with visitors regularly crossing to picnic on the Bass Rock. To cater for the demand and provide more acceptable accommodation a new hotel was built close to the road, overlooking the bay below, and which continued trading until 1920.

In 1922 the Dalrymple family put Canty Bay and its properties on the market for sale and although it fell through, it was remarketed the following year when it was bought in September by William Edgar Evans. Evans, a botanist, naturalist and photographer, purchased the property for the use of scouts - mainly the group associated with the Charlotte Baptist Church, Edinburgh, of which he was scoutmaster. Today the properties – the converted hotel and cottages – are still well used throughout the summer months by visiting scouts and other youth groups.

Above Left : Postcard of Canty Bay Hotel used by R. Kirkpatrick, Lessee, to advise prospective clients of his terms - Lunch 1/6d; Tea 9d. c1906
Above Right : Scouts boarding steam launch 'Bonnie Doon' for trip to the Bass Rock. c1922

Golf

Golf in North Berwick was played on the Town Common as early as the seventeenth century, the game being recorded in the Kirk Session minutes of 1605. But it was not until 1832 that a club, the North Berwick Golf Club, was formed to play over a 'green' in the west of the town, the West Links. Originally over six holes, from Elcho Green to the March dyke, the course was, over the next one hundred years or so, extended over Ferrygate and Archerfield land to make a course of 18 holes, whose attractiveness is almost without equal yet providing the sternest test for the most proficient golfer, and with two of the most famous holes in golf, 'Redan' and 'Perfection'. It was not until 1879 when the idea for a proper clubhouse was given serious consideration – until then a tent had been used – and only then to assuage those dissenting the proposal, it was necessary to form another club – the New Club. The clubhouse was formally opened the following year.

During the last quarter of the nineteenth century, with fishing in decline, many fishermen and their sons turned to caddying to help make a living. The game already popular with the aristocracy and gentry was becoming increasingly popular with the middle classes. Easily accessible by rail, the town became a popular destination to play the Royal game from April through to September with caddies finding regular 'carries', often carrying clubs for the same golfers, year after year.

Such could be the rapport between caddie and player that strong relationships built up between them over many years. 'Big' Henry Crawford was one such caddy. Large, quick-witted and loyal with an endearing personality, he regularly carried for Ben Sayers in his 'big stake' matches. A. J. Balfour, as government minister and later Prime Minister, was another of his regulars he loyally caddied for, even carrying for him at St Andrews when Balfour was appointed captain

Top : The new clubhouse with smart entrance porch. To the rear, right, can be seen the gasometer and in the centre, behind the porch, Point Garry Cottage, later to become clubhouse for the Tantallon Golf Club. c1880
Above : Sitting patiently hoping for a carry, this group of caddies, mostly local fishermen, wait outside the caddymaster's box at the West Links. c1900

of the 'R and A' in 1894. Crawford's loyalty to Balfour continued long after he retired and took charge of the gingerbeer hut at the far end of the course. The 'Sportsman' once told a story of when Grand Duke Michael of Russia was playing the course and on approaching the refreshment stall was grateful to see it bedecked with bunting and flags. 'Its very kind of you, Crawford,' he said appreciatively, as he gave his order, 'to have the decorations out for me.' 'Na, na, Mr. Michael,' replied Crawford, who always addressed the Grand Duke this way, 'they're for a better man than you. They're for Mr. Balfour!'

Many caddies took up the game itself with many others taking-up clubmaking apprenticeships. Some eventually turned professional, and many of those ventured overseas to seek their fortune in Europe, America, South Africa and Australia, pioneering their sport and spreading its gospel, contributing significantly to the sport's eventual global popularity. And from amongst their ranks came winners of the Open and US Open. In 1904 both championships on either side of the Atlantic were won by North Berwick men – Willie Anderson the US Open, which he won four times, and Jack White, winner of 'The Open'.

'Stake' or 'challenge' matches were a regular sight on the 'greens' particularly towards the end of the nineteenth century. Usually played on a 'home and home' basis with either 18 or 36 holes over a player's home course and the same number over the opponent's home

Above : 'Big' Crawford was a giant of a man with a reputation for his rugged outspokenness but he could still command considerable respect from both his fellow caddies and golfers alike. 1900

Right : Norman Grant, driver, in Cannes. He was one of the many professional golfers, born and raised in North Berwick, who helped spread the sport of golf world-wide. Grant first worked in Argentina before moving to France in 1927 when he was appointed professional at the Cannes Country Club.

course, and sometimes for a purse of as much as £100. Park played with Vardon over 72 holes at North Berwick and Ganton in 1899 for £200 and a match could attract many hundreds of spectators.

In 1894 a new nine-hole course, the Rhodes, was opened in the east of the Burgh in response to the cry of overcrowding on the West Links. Unfortunately the course was not a commercial success, failing to attract enough members and with too few visitors, sadly closed a few years later. Later, with the increasing pressure which popularity brought to the West Links, a new attempt was made to open a course in the east of the town. In 1908 the new 18 hole Corporation Golf Course with its breathtaking cliff top location and spectacular views over the Firth of Forth and its islands was opened. Laid out by James Braid and Ben Sayers, it was opened with a professional tournament which included J H Taylor, Sandy Herd, Andra Kirkcaldy and Ben Sayers.

With its first class reputation, golf at North Berwick thrived with, in particular, the West Links attracting ever-increasing numbers of the middle classes. By the 1920s, the West Links was a Mecca for golf. The ground around Dan Stephen's starter's box was crowded with titled and society players from both home and abroad, anxious to play the West Links. The sports and society pages of magazines and newspapers of the day regularly ran articles and accompanying photographs about the golf at North Berwick enticing many more to visit the Royal Burgh, and not just for golf.

Golf has played a significant part in North Berwick's history, and North Berwick has played a significant part in the history of the game of golf.

Above : Part of the large crowd enjoying one of the many tussles between Ben Sayers and Andra' Kirkaldy. The match over 36 holes for a purse of money, subscribed by visiting and resident gentlemen, was won by Kirkaldy by two holes. August 1897
Below : Greenkeepers on the Corporation Golf Course, now the Glen Golf Club, with push mowers and horse-drawn fairway mower. c1925
Page opposite : The world famous 15th Tee, 'Redan,' on the West Links. c1934

North Berwick Railway Station

In December 1843 the North British Railway Company (NBRC) held a public meeting in North Berwick to gauge support for a line to run from the London-Edinburgh mainline to connect with the town. Over the course of the next few years there was much debate as to where the line would terminate and which route it would take. One of the original ideas was to carry the line all the way down to the harbour - along the west bay with arches over the likes of the slaughterhouse (site of Hope Rooms) and down to the Platcock Rocks – later shorted to end at Shore Street (now Victoria Road). By 1845 this proposal had been discarded in favour of a line running along the south part of the town and eastwards to Seacliff where the building of a village was being considered. At the same time a further plan by the Scottish District Northern Railway Company proposed incorporating the line with a ferry to Elie to connect with trains from Dundee and the north. In the end, the line terminated near where it ends today and was opened in summer 1850, bringing with it easier access to a growing demand from visitors, and new jobs in new professions and trades – engine drivers and stokers, railway guards, carters and porters and surfacemen.

New arrivals by train in the early 1850s, were met with a very different view to what we see today. Disembarking from the train, exiting the station and crossing the track a visitor would have been standing on the edge of a gentle ridge. Below lay the higgledy-piggledy layout of North Berwick, which, apart from the gas works on the West Links belching out its dirty black smoke; Bridges iron foundry behind the newly built Quadrant; and the new developments being carried out on the East Bay, was much as it had been for generations.

Looking around, our passenger would be aware that there were few buildings at his elevation or higher other than the farm buildings of the Abbey and Mains farms, the ruins of the old Abbey, and the Napoleonic lookout post on top of the Law. There was no Royal Hotel, no York Road, no Dirleton Avenue, only fields. Down below the entrance to the west of the town, at the Toll House, now the site of the North Berwick Golf Club.

By the mid-Victorian period organised train trips were bringing large influxes of excursionists to the town. Each train could disgorge many hundreds of day-trippers all ready to invade the town like a swarm of locusts – eating and drinking the town bare. The 'Courier' in 1874 reported 'the bakers' and confectioners' shops were harried of their contents; soda water was not to be had for love or money, and the publicans were never so brisk, though none were compelled to shut their doors.' They came from far and near – Perth, Coatbridge, Glasgow, Hawick, West Benhar, and Burntisland - many accompanied by their own brass band, and representing all sorts of employment including miners, iron workers, woollen mill workers and employees of the Co-operative Society.

In 1879, following requests from wealthy Edinburgh golfers, who were as a consequence of the crowded nature of the golfing links, unable to complete a full round during the darker spring months using the ordinary train service, North British Railways (NBR) agreed to run a special golfers' express every Saturday between February and May, provided they received a guarantee from fifty subscribers to the series of eighteen trains for which a subscription of £2 was charged.

However in the eyes of the Town Council, the arrival of the train was not without its problems. In 1874 the Town Council wrote to the NBR regarding the 'injury which excursion parties were doing to the town as a Watering Place both by reason of their number and size' petitioning the directors to put some restriction on these excursions

Excursion trip pamphlet for the employees of The Burntisland Oil Company Limited, candleworks division. 16th June 1888

The Burntisland Oil Company held their first excursionist trip to North Berwick on Saturday 16 June 1888. The trip, for the employees of the firm's candleworks in Kinghorn would have been paid for by the company and likely to be the employees only real day of holiday. They had to take the train-ferry across the five-mile stretch of the Forth from Burntisland to Granton and from there into the city of Edinburgh to catch the train to North Berwick. The excursionists might take a morning walk along the High Street before taking in the sights at the harbour and perhaps watch a paddle-steamer collecting a few wealthy passengers, before setting sail for the Bass and May islands, then dinner at John Sawyers "Tower of Babel" temperance establishment on Quality Street. Served by Sawyer and his wife and two eldest daughters, the party would enjoy a lunch of local produce before setting off to the East Links for games and dancing. The occasion would certainly have been a day that the workers looked forward to for many months beforehand and remembered for many months afterwards.

for the future if the 'prosperity and progress of the Burgh is to be maintained'.

Conversely, by the early years of the new century the Town Council were in regular correspondence with NBR encouraging them to lay on more trains during the summer season particularly the 'Lothian Coast Express' – the service that allowed the head of the household to return to work for the second fortnight of the holiday while wife and family enjoyed their stay in North Berwick. It began in June 1912 as a NBR summer express running from June through to September between Glasgow Queen Street and the resorts of Dunbar, North Berwick and Gullane. Called the 'Lothian Coast Express' the three-carriage-train left Dunbar at 7.55am and collected a further three and two carriages at Drem and Longniddry stations respectively - the North Berwick and Gullane sections that had been delivered by their own independent engine. The train, combined, proceeded to Waverley and then through to Glasgow arriving at Queen Street at 9.49am and running weekdays only so it was particularly suited to the West Coast businessman. The return commute left Glasgow at 3.50pm. Dining facilities were available, which at the time was very rare, although they were abandoned in 1920. The 'Lothian Coast Express' continued providing seasonal service until 1932 with a break only during the latter years of the First War.

Today, despite, the serious threat of closure of the line and station in 1968, the demolition of the station buildings and shortening of the line by 50 yards in 1985, the railway line to North Berwick still provides an invaluable asset to the community and those along its length and the trains using it continue to deliver thousands of visitors to the town each year.

Top : North Berwick station staff, including the manager, cashier, porters, and shop staff. c1920
Bottom : Bill boards promoting the benefits of North Berwick and its accessibility by train. c1911

24

The Lothian Coast Express, engine Reid 4-4-0 No.359 'Dirk Hatteraick', standing at North Berwick c1922

Steam train departing North Berwick station with goods yard and sidings (centre) and Bass Rock in the distance. c1950

Any visitor arriving at North Berwick by train in the late 40s, 50s and early 60s could not fail to appreciate the labour of love put in to creating the prize-winning bedding displays by porter Darling Runciman (right). And today, visitors have a similar visual treat organised by 'North Berwick In Bloom' with bright and colourful raised beds, planters and two-wheeled props (below).

Darling Runciman (right) started with the railway at North Berwick in 1919, firstly in the goods yard and later as a porter. When in the 1940s he took over responsibility for the station garden, North Berwick appeared on the prize list of "Best Kept Station Gardens' every year until Darling's retirement in the 1960s. The first award was a modest Third Class but progress was steady until, during the 1950s, seven Special Class Awards were won including four accredited with special "A". With up to 10,000 plants planted annually, there was always work to be done - from soil preparation at the end of the year, sowing seeds in January, planting in April and May, and pruning, dead-heading and weeding throughout the summer and autumn.

New Hotels and Property to Let

The growth of North Berwick as a summer destination, like other resorts, developed side by side with the increase in hotel accommodation. Although served by a small number of inns and boarding establishments in the first half of the eighteenth century – Dalrymple Hotel, Commercial Hotel, and Ship Inn - none could offer accommodation of the style and elegance so desired by the wealthy visitor. It was the opening of the Royal Hotel in 1861, a building funded by a group of wealthy investors, when the requirements of the wealthy classes were first provided for – sumptuous furnishings and fittings, discreet service, and a magnificent view over the golfing links, the west bay, and harbour with the Bass Rock in the distance. Within a couple of years the original building was extended twice to cater for the demand and by 1873 was promoting itself as 'one of most complete Provincial Hotels in the Kingdom,' replete with all modern appliances.

MARINE HOTEL, NORTH BERWICK.
C. C. HUGHES, Manager

The Royal was soon joined by a number of Private Hotels with most, as made clear in their trade adverts, 'looking to secure the patronage of the Nobility and Gentry.' In 1876 they were joined by the Marine Hotel. The hotel, owned by the North Berwick Marine Hotel Company, was funded through public subscription by a diverse group of shareholders from North Berwick and Edinburgh including merchants, a lawyer, painters, a clergyman, and a tax collector. The hotel was built in the Scots baronial style to cater for the burgeoning number of visitors from the upper classes, providing every convenience known to man including salt and fresh water baths, both hot and cold. Sadly the original building was destroyed by fire in 1882.

Fortunately the proprietors were insured and its replacement was open for business little more than a year after the fire. Further hotels were built to satisfy an endless demand: Warrender House, Tantallon Lodge, Bradbury, Lenheim Park, Imperial and many more including Tantallon Hall in 1908, the last of the great hotels to be built.

Above : Tantallon Hall - the last of the large purpose-built hotels in North Berwick. c1922
Right : Chamber Pot from the Marine Hotel c1900. Amongst the many duties carried out by chamber maids were those connected with chamber pots. It must have been one of the more unpleasant tasks particularly during the Victorian Period when plumbing was rather rudimentary.
Top Right : Trade adverts from 1878
Previous Page : Advert showing the original Marine Hotel building, sadly destroyed by fire in 1882.

As well as hotel accommodation, the spate of house building for absentee owners over the second half of the eighteenth century meant that their properties were available for let outwith their period of occupation. Local agents, of which there were many in the town – including shopkeepers Edington's, Shiels', Wightman's and joiners Auld's and Denholm - were employed to oversee the lettings and many were charged with looking after the property during the off-season. This would often include overseeing essential maintenance, repair work and the vital airing of the property before the start of the season when a retinue of staff could be expected to arrive.

In George Shiel and Sons' 1907 'Up-to-Date Guide to North Berwick', as well as 14 hotels listed there were 242 private houses and apartments to be had. All properties came with servants' rooms and a few available with service if required. In addition there were a further 100 properties available for let with attendance. No figures are available for the occupancy levels of the accommodation available but given the number available demand must have strong, and this is borne out in the visitor lists published regularly in the local press. The list published for North Berwick in the 30th August 1907 edition of the *Haddington Advertiser* names 236 houses along with their summer tenants and seven hotels with a total of over 260 guests. Not all accommodation is listed and no allowance is given to the size of party. On 10 and 11 August 1918, during the Great War when the levels of visitors were significantly lower, a census carried out by the Town Council reported that there were 2505 residents and 3311 visitors staying in the town and that both before and after the War it can be safely assumed, with day trippers, the number of people in the town could comfortably exceed 10,000.

Trade adverts for house agents M & A Edington c1930 (left), George Ferrier c1873 (below) and George Shiel & Sons (right) c1896.

Telegrams: "Edington North Berwick"

ESTABLISHED 1823

Telephone: North Berwick 1

HOUSE AGENTS

Full information Free regarding Furnished Houses or Apartments will be forwarded on application

ITALIAN WAREHOUSEMEN

High-Class Grocers, Tea, Coffee and Wine Merchants

Our policy is to sell only such Merchandise as we can unreservedly recommend and guarantee, at the Lowest Prices known for such qualities, and to maintain a service in keeping with the character of our Merchandise and Patronage

M. & A. EDINGTON
89-61 High Street, North Berwick

Furnished Lodgings - 1873

PARTIES having such to Let, and those in quest of the same ought to communicate at once with GEORGE FERRIER, House Agent, Quality Street, who from his long experience in the line guarantees to fix people comfortably and economically on shortest notice, Houses from £4 to £50 per month, according to size, position, &c., great choice. To save trouble kindly state accommodation required and amount of Rental. Two commodious Farm Houses with Stabling, &c., on Lists at moderate rates.

LICENSED HOUSE AGENT AND
APPRAISER
QUALITY STREET, NORTH BERWICK.

HOUSE AGENCY DEPARTMENT.

Publishers of the

UP-TO-DATE GUIDE TO NORTH BERWICK
AND LIST OF FURNISHED HOUSES AND APARTMENTS TO LET.

With Coloured Plan of Town. 120 Pages. Illustrated.

Contains Particulars regarding all Letting Houses in the Town.
Gratis and Post Free.

Intending Visitors are invited to communicate with us regarding the accommodation they require. Full Information and complete List of available Houses and Rooms, with Plan showing situations, sent on request. Every Assistance rendered in making selection.

No Charges in this Department.

GEO. SHIEL & SONS,
82 & 84 High St. (Next Post Office)
· NORTH BERWICK·

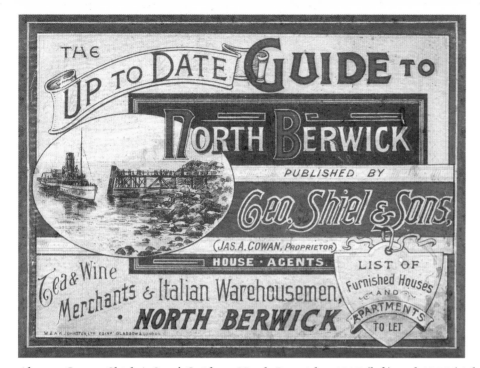

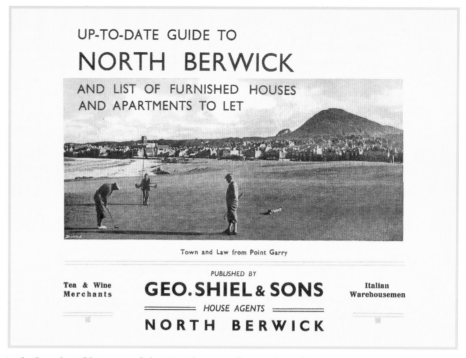

Above : George Shiel & Sons' Guide to North Berwick - 1907 (left) and 1926 (right) They include a brief history of the Burgh as well as a list of its amenities and the many attractions that might interest the summer visitor as well as lengthy lists of accommodation to let. Among the many different types of property available in the 1907 Guide are 242 private houses available to let.

Below : By the late 1920s, Edington's guides were being published without lists of accommodation and were more about extolling the wonderful amenities North Berwick had to offer, including the shops where they naturally placed their own fine establishment at 89 & 91 High Street centre-stage.

North Berwick Lifeboat

In December 1859 the North Berwick Town Council considered the contents of a letter from Richard Lewis, Secretary of the RNLI, regarding a Lifeboat being stationed in the town. Mr Lewis intimated that a benevolent gentleman from London had offered to defray the cost of the lifeboat and its equipment which was expected to amount to £180. The cost of a suitable boat-house was expected to cost a further £120 and Mr Lewis in his letter requested the assistance of local parties to raise the monies, intimating that they would also require a further £20 a year to cover the costs of the coxswain's salary, and the crew for exercising every quarter. The cost of the transporting carriage was to be borne by the lifeboat institution.

The rocks in the seas around North Berwick had caused many ships to flounder – many with the loss of life. Only a few months before Mr Lewis's letter, two ships were wrecked in close proximity to the town, with one, the *Bubona*, wrecked just to the west of Canty Bay resulting in the death of its crew.

The Council resolved to make a site available at the bottom of Shore Street (now Victoria Road) near the harbour, with no feu duty or rent charged. A local branch of the RNLI was quickly established and by the autumn of 1860 had raised over £200. By early the following year a six-oared single banked self-righting lifeboat, complete with full equipment and transporting carriage had been supplied to North Berwick. The boat's name was

'Caroline' and she gave service for seven years. She was followed by a further six lifeboats - Caroline II, Freemason, Fergus Ferguson, Norman Clark, John William Dudley and Elizabeth Moore Garden before the station closed at the end of 1925. In total the seven boats were launched 37 times and saved 64 lives.

Lifeboat 'Elizabeth Moore Garden' during celebrations for the RNLI centenary 1924

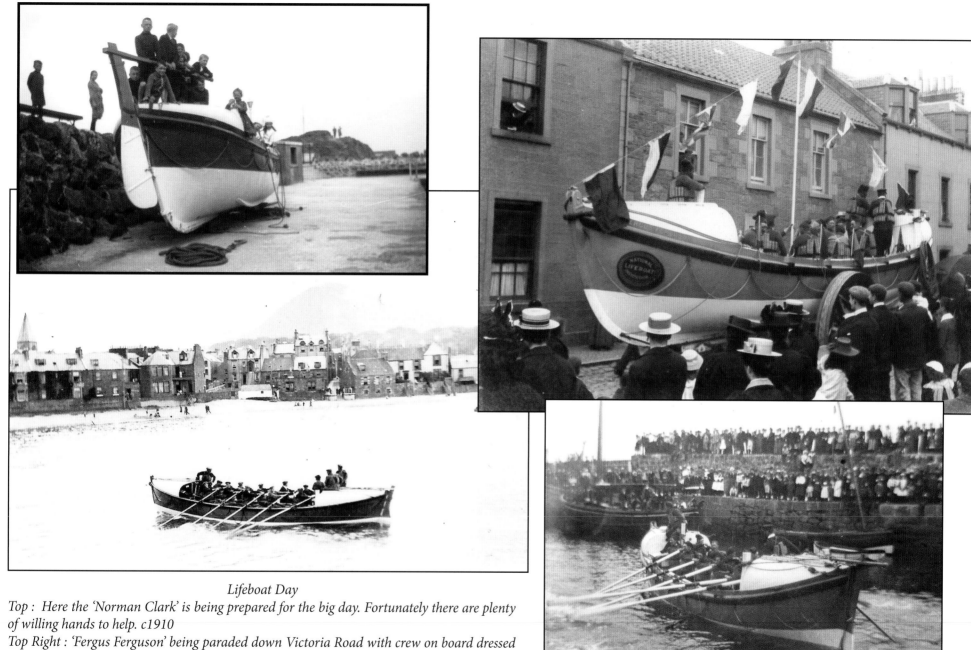

Lifeboat Day

Top : Here the 'Norman Clark' is being prepared for the big day. Fortunately there are plenty of willing hands to help. c1910

Top Right : 'Fergus Ferguson' being paraded down Victoria Road with crew on board dressed in their cork waistcoats and guernseys taking the applause from grateful bystanders. c1900

Above and Right : Demonstration of the lifeboat's ability in the West Bay and harbour. c1900

There was no lifeboat stationed at North Berwick again until 1966 when the BBC's children's programme 'Blue Peter' presented 'Blue Peter III', an inshore lifeboat, to Sir Hew Hamilton Dalrymple as President of the North Berwick RNLI.

Initially stationed in the Old Granary, the lifeboat was rehoused in the original lifeboat building in 1991, and remains there today when not out on call.

A regular feature of the summer in North Berwick has been the Lifeboat Fete or Lifeboat Day as it is sometimes called, which is the main annual fund-raising event in aid of the lifeboat. Over the years the skills of the service have been demonstrated to many hundreds of spectators who annually support the event. Originally this would include a parade through the town with the lifeboat on its carriage and the crew dressed in cork waistcoats and red cowl guernseys seated inside. Subsequently the boat would be launched and an exhibition given in the bay. Over the years the arrangements for the day have varied and included driving displays, dances in the Pavilion, Mrs Keith's fetes in Dirleton, free film screening at the Playhouse by Mr Scott, all helping to make the event enjoyable and remarkably successful in the amount of funds raised. Today the lifeboat is often joined by the 'Trent' class lifeboat from Dunbar and a Sea King air sea rescue helicopter. More recently the fete has moved to Elcho Green because space at the harbour is at a premium.

Above : The official handing over of Blue Peter III on 6th May 1969 by Lady Anne-Louise Hamilton Dalrymple, here presented with a bouquet of thanks by Miss Pat Marr.

The IRB Crew 1969

A Russell T Brown W Brunton J McHenry S Auld D Stewart J Robertson M McVicar N Pugh T Cunningham R Thorburn

B Pearson B Millar G Thorburn D Tweedie N Chisholm W Macnair D Millar J Pearson N Butterworth

Royal National **Lifeboat** Institution

52-12

NORTH BERWICK
CARNIVAL

CARNIVAL PARADE	9.30	Children's Fancy Dress
	11.15	Diving Display
	12.50	The Band of the Scots Guards
CARNIVAL SHOWGROUND	14.00	Opening Ceremony

- The Royal Navy • Royal Tank Regiment • 42nd Field Artillery Regiment
- The Royal Air Force • The RNLI • HM Coast Guard
- The Band of The Regimental Scots Guards
- North Berwick Pipe Band
- Lothian & Borders Regional Fire Brigade
- SSEB • British Telecom
- Vintage Agricultural Machinery
- BMX

SATURDAY 26th. JULY 1986

ALL DAY FUN !

Stalls Galore!

• LUCKY PROGRAMME •
British Caledonian & London Hilton Hotel
Weekend Break for Two People & £100 cash!

Clockwise from Above : Lifeboat Day poster 1986; Lifeboat Day at the harbour 1970s and Lifeboat Day at the harbour 1950s.

North Berwick Bowling Club

Opening of the Green at the south west end of Quality Street July 1865

In 1865 another attraction was added to North Berwick's repertoire with the formation of a bowling green at the south end of Quality Street on ground granted for the purpose by Sir Hew Dalrymple. Work was quickly commenced to turn what was previously a kitchen garden into a green which was both desirable to both residents and visitors.

The ground was thoroughly drained and turf laid over successive layers of soil, sea marl, and ashes so as to secure the driest possible surface. An ample supply of turf was supplied by Mr Laidlay of Seacliff and the Right Hon. R.C. Hamilton, with the cartage carried out by several neighbouring farmers. The green measured 120 feet by 70 feet with the utmost care taken to ensure its perfect flatness. A neat house was erected in the south-west corner of the green whilst a lofty flag pole was erected opposite, on which a Union Jack was to be unfurled when members were at play. The whole expense of the green was £61 10 shillings – the green £51 and flags and bowls £6 10 shillings. The costs were met from voluntary subscriptions £31; 45 annual subscribers at 10 shillings – being 7s 6d entry and 2s 6d annual dues. This left a deficit of £8 which, it was hoped, would be covered by further subscriptions. The green was opened in July 1865 to an assembly of invited guests and under the musical direction of a band from Edinburgh.

By the start of the Edwardian era the Green was no longer felt adequate for its purpose mainly because it was unable to accommodate the large number of visitors wishing to play during the summer season, and as it was not practical to enlarge it, a new site on the south side of Clifford road was secured. Opened in May 1904, the new Green was laid out with beautiful turf from Lunan Bay, Montrose with an attractive pavilion and offices adjacent. Some years later a second green was added to the west.

During the summer season the greens were a popular location with visitors, particularly during the Glasgow fortnight, and such popularity brought much needed prosperity to the club.

Opening of the new Green on the south side of Clifford Road. May 1904

Children's Golf Competitions

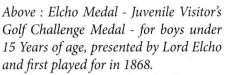

Children's golf tournaments started in North Berwick in 1867 with a competition for the sons of visitors, organised by Mr Smith Sligo. The next year, following the tournament's success, Lord Elcho offered a handsome silver medal, the Juvenile Visitor's Golf Challenge Medal. Possibly the first such medal offered in the world of golf, it was to be competed for annually by boys under the age of 15, the winner having the best handicap score over a round of the West Links. The first winner was A. Peacock with a net round of 36.

That same year, 1868, Mrs Nelson, wife of the Edinburgh publisher, organised a second tournament for boys, again sons of visitors, by offering a set of prize clubs for the competition, which attracted 37 handicapped players. On the same day a competition over the short holes was played by the young lady visitors. For 1869 the Elcho Medal was played over the newly extended course of 10 holes, with younger players under ten years of age playing over the short or 'Ladies' Course'.

A new tournament was organised in 1883 for 'Young Gentlemen Residenters' the first competition purely for locals boys - albeit in the main the sons of merchants and professionals. Over the next 70 years or so a number of competitions were started – the Cree Medal, the Balfour Melville Trophy and the Hume Cup to name a few – to be competed for by children of all ages and of both sexes and from all backgrounds.

Above : Elcho Medal - Juvenile Visitor's Golf Challenge Medal - for boys under 15 Years of age, presented by Lord Elcho and first played for in 1868.
Right : A few sons of well-off parents receiving tuition from local professionals David Grant and Ben Sayers. c1890

In 1935 the West Links played host to the first Scottish Boys' Golf Championship – a competition inaugurated by the North Berwick Golf Club. A gold medal for the winner was presented by Mr R. J. Addie, Captain of the New Golf Club, with a silver medal for the runner-up presented by General A. Blair and bronze medals for the semi-finalists gifted by Mr Robert Maxwell and Captain J. B. Whitelaw. Forty-seven entries were received for the first tournament with David Blair, the son of a regular summer visiting family to the town and a member of North Berwick Club, declared the first winner. For the next forty years the championship was played each April over the town course, but only once producing a local winner, 16 year-old Brian Thomson in 1952, a club-maker with Ben Sayers and member of the Bass Rock G.C. All square after 36 holes, Thomson overcame his opponent, 17 year-old Inverness Academy pupil Ian Rodger, on the second extra hole.

The Malcolm Cup, previously called the Milton Lodge Cup, originated in 1973 and is held annually in August. It is open to all children under 14 years, with any competitor who reaches a score of 10 on any one hole carefully manoeuvred on to the next hole. The competition is held over one round of stroke play on the morning of competition, with the best 8 to play in a knockout that same afternoon with numerous prizes given out to the competitors. Started as a fund-raiser, the competition has, to date, raised in excess of £14000 for various charities and local good causes.

Below : Brian Thomson with the Scottish Boys' Golf Championship trophy. 1952
Right : Enthusiastic competitors in the Malcolm Cup, including a future Ladies' Open Champion receiving her prize (Below centre). 1980s

Paddle Steamers of the Forth

Regular sightings of steamers off the coast of North Berwick were first recorded in the 1830s. However, it was over thirty years later in 1866 when the Newcastle firm of Steedman, Hanson & Dykes started a regular run to North Berwick with their tug 'Powerful.' Sailing from Leith every Thursday throughout the season of 1866, this was the first regular excursion to North Berwick and the outer Forth, finishing up at May Island. The sailings to North Berwick became increasingly popular as the town's reputation as a place to be seen grew. By June 1875 the same firm, with its newly commissioned vessel 'May', started its summer campaign with a trip from North Berwick to Dundee, which by the end of the month, included the May Island. (A few years later on this cruise, passengers could view the construction of the Tay Rail Bridge before taking a stroll around the busy and prosperous streets of Dundee.) However that summer the firm faced competition from George Jamieson's tug, the 'Fiery Cross', with its sailings between Leith and the May which took in all the intervening coastal ports, including the Royal Burgh, on the way. Further competition in the late 1870s prevented Dykes from making a commercial success of the outer Forth routes and the firm closed its Forth operations – effectively giving Jamieson a monopoly on the run. Despite the 'Fiery Cross's' lack of sophistication she was a popular craft with excursionists - Jamieson was able to poke the bow of the tug into the rocks of the May enabling the passengers a couple of hours ashore. The 'Fiery Cross's' size and manoeuvrability ensured safe landing at the

Stirling Castle departing North Berwick c1900

Above : Advert from the Haddingtonshire Courier 3 June 1881
Right : Steamer off the Bass Rock c1900

Platcock Rocks, North Berwick where other larger steamers found difficulty, particularly in low water or in difficult swells.

The increasing popularity of cruising encouraged the arrival of larger steamships with sumptuous saloons and dining facilities. However their size limited the ports they were able to call at. North Berwick was particularly difficult and in April 1886 a letter of request from Mr M. P. Galloway, managing director of The Galloway Saloon Steam Packet Company (G.S.S.P.), was laid before the Town Council, to erect a pier at the Platcock Rocks. In his letter, which was accompanied with sketch plans, Galloway confirmed that the 115 lineal feet construction which was to extend in a northerly direction, would not interfere with the navigation of the harbour; that its intended use was for his steamers alone, and that there would be no Sunday calls at the pier. The pier allowed passengers to board and disembark at three levels thereby ensuring access to the steamers whatever the level of water. The Council, at a special meeting convened the following week, approved the plans and proposals giving Galloway a 21-year lease at an annual rent of £5 but subject to him paying all construction costs and all future maintenance expenses. At the end of each season the wooden gangways were to be removed and stored. Unfortunately, due to the late delivery of iron and a poor subsea survey, the pier was not opened until 25 May 1888 following which the Magistrates and Town Councillors of the Burgh enjoyed a trip to Elie on board Mr Galloway's steamer the 'S.S. Stirling Castle'.

For the next thirty seasons or so G.S.S.P.'s steamers, The 'Stirling Castle', 'Tantallon Castle' and 'The Redgauntlet' ferried excursionists

Above : For this excursion the upper deck of this steamer is filled with passengers with the trip for many being the highlight of their summer holiday. c1900

Left : Ferrying passengers aboard a steamer by tender with Craigleith in the distance. c1900

Below : Galloway's Advert from c1890.

from port to port, and to and around the islands of the Forth. The vessels were lavishly furnished and decorated and lit with modern electric lighting. Brass bands would entertain during the trip and when the steamer moored at North Berwick the band would march up to the High Street alerting people a steamer was in town and about to leave. Fares, although only a shilling or two with luncheon and teas extra, were beyond the pocket of the working man so it was an experience for the wealthy visitor and growing middle classes from Edinburgh, Fife and the Lothians. By the turn of the century the increasingly affluent middle classes were starting to emulate their wealthier peers by taking holidays to the favoured spa towns around the country. Taking a trip on board a steamer would allow them to see the islands of the Forth and the towns and ports along its shore and also, but just as importantly, allow them to be seen too, promenading along the shore, sipping a lemonade, or sitting on the newly sited benches on the harbour wall watching the steamers' comings and goings.

Steamboat Pier, North Berwick.

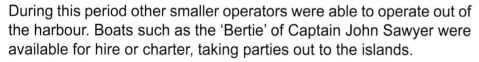

Above : Steamboat collecting passengers from Galloway's Pier. Boarding was possible at one or two of the three levels depending on the tide. c1900
Left : Redgauntlet approaching Galloway's Pier.

During this period other smaller operators were able to operate out of the harbour. Boats such as the 'Bertie' of Captain John Sawyer were available for hire or charter, taking parties out to the islands.

The start of the First War saw the end of all excursions on the Forth when restrictions were placed on the movement of all marine vessels by the Commander-in-Chief, The Nore. The public traffic regulations which were overseen by 'The King's Harbourmaster,' Rosyth, included pilotage for all but the smallest craft. In any case a number of the paddle steamers were requisitioned by the Admiralty for wartime duties – mainly minesweeping. It was the end of an era: steam paddleboats carrying excursionists around the Forth were never to return to North Berwick. It was not until the twenties that smaller, privately owned motor launches started taking passengers from North Berwick out into the Forth and round its islands.

In 1919 Galloway's Pier was put up for sale but found no takers. Over the next twenty years the Town Council endeavoured to put the pier to good use with little reward. Eventually, with an eye for the need for iron to aid the war effort, the Town Council contacted Mr William Finlayson, Musselburgh to remove the metal from the jetty to the specifications laid down by Mr Robertson, the Burgh Engineer. Finlayson's offer of £10 was accepted with the cement left clean. Today the foundations are still to be seen and are all that is left as a memorial to the bygone days of steamers at North Berwick.

Left : Steamer with its passengers crowding the decks as it approaches Galloway's Pier.
Above : Tantallon Castle off the Platcock Rocks.
Previous Page : Red Gauntlet moored at May Island.

c1900

TRIAL TRIP OF THE TANTALLON CASTLE. – On Saturday forenoon the pleasure saloon steamer, 'Tantallon Castle', which was launched from the yard of Messrs S. H. Morton, shipbuilders Leith, about the beginning of last month went on her official trial trip. The vessel is built for the Galloway Saloon Steam Packet Company – the company being induced to make an addition to their fleet from the increasing popularity of the summer trips on the Firth of Forth. For a correct proof of the vessel's speed, a strong easterly breeze, causing a heavy ground swell, proved very unfavourable, but notwithstanding this she covered the measured mile at Gullane at the rate of 15 knots an hour, which was considered very satisfactory. Her dimensions are as follows:- Length, 198ft.; breadth, 21ft.; depth, 8ft. 6in.; and she is built of mild steel. The furnishings of the interior are on a most elaborate scale, everything, in fact, being so arranged as to secure the utmost comfort to the passenger. The main saloon deck, with ladies' saloon adjoining, are tastefully upholstered in old gold plush, and the former room is beautifully finished in carved teak wood. Immediately below the main saloon is situated a spacious, well-ventilated dining cabin, laid in crimson cloth, with tables in the centre, and seated [sic] for nearly 100 persons. In the fore cabin there is another dining apartment for steerage passengers. The vessel is fitted throughout with electric light, supplied by an iron-clad dynamo driven by an Archer engine. There are 30 incandescent lights of 20 candle-power each and a bridge lamp to allow the passengers landing with safety on returning from evening cruises. The engines of the Tantallon Castle, supplied by the builders, are on the single diagonal surface-condensing principle, having a cylinder 45 inches in diameter, 5 feet 6 inches stroke, deriving their motive power from a verticle steam boiler. After sailing the measured mile at Gullane on Saturday, the vessel steamed up the Firth and in smoother waters luncheon was served to the company and among the number of toasts proposed were those of success to the new steamer and the health of the manager of the company, Mr M. P. Galloway.

North Berwick Advertiser June 1887

Ben Sayers

Rosie Neuman, the London socialite and amateur film-maker was a regular summer visitor to North Berwick during the twenties and thirties. A keen golfer, she could be seen almost daily on the West Links during her stays there. She epitomised the upper-class visitor to North Berwick at that time as she was from a well-connected family who were extremely wealthy and she had a passion for golf. In her memoirs she captures the mood of the period 'on entering Mr. Sayers' shop at the West Links, one's whole existence seemed to be transformed – worries were all forgotten. All that mattered was golf, and to be on one's game was utopia.'

During the summer season, particularly around mid-morning, the golfers among the wealthy visitors would congregate around the first tee on the West Links awaiting their tee-time. During the season much of London Society, including most of the nobility of Britain

with many more from Europe, the owners and the heirs of the most prestigious merchant banks, industrialists from home and abroad, politicians and members of His Majesty's government and various others with the requisite connections, could be seen on the West Links. There, luncheons and dinner parties could be discussed, business strategies gone over and compared, political manoeuvering agreed, even consideration to the likely changes in the next cabinet reshuffle.

Part of their holiday experience was reacquainting themselves with the Sayers, both 'Wee Ben' and his son, 'Young Ben', their staff, Dan Stephen the starter, and the caddies. Within the Sayers' emporium at the West Links, players could resolve all difficulties with their game – clubs could be adjusted, lessons arranged, stances and grips tweaked, nothing was ever too much trouble.

Ben Sayers' first premises at the West Links was a box at Inchgarry overlooking what is now the seventeenth tee. Erected in the 1890s and built with pitch-pine, the flat-roofed affair gave Sayers his first opportunity to sell his wares - clubs, balls and lessons - directly to passing golfers.

Far Left : Outside his box at Inchgarry, Ben Sayers (note his jacket pockets bulging with golf balls) with his wife's nephews, Sonny and Arthur Grant, left and right respectively, both of whom became professionals. 1910

Left : Inside Sayers' golf club and ball maker's box at Inchgarry where a large collection of clubs can been seen either for sale or, having been altered, for collection by their owner. Along the left wall are a number of lockers - presumably for Sayers' regular customers. 1897

Previous page : Ben Sayers Snr c1914
Below, this and previous page : View to Craigleith with Ben Sayers' shop (left) and caddies' and starter's boxes centre right. The pitched roofs of the bathing boxes can be seen peeking above the edge of the West Links. c1921
Right : Sayers' advert from 1898.

B. SAYERS,
Winner of 22 first-class Tournaments.

Championship Golf Balls.

GOLF CLUB AND BALL MANUFACTURER
(Wholesale and Export).

☞ *Clubs supplied to Royalty.*

LINKS, NORTH BERWICK

Ben Sayers, or 'Wee Ben' as he was affectionately called, was born in Leith in 1856, and first came to North Berwick in about 1880. He slowly built his reputation as a fine professional, winning many tournaments - although he never won the Open despite competing in over forty Championships between 1880 and 1923. It was when playing in head to head matches, either singly or in pairs, and when representing his country - representing Scotland each year between 1903 and 1913 - that he earned such a formidable, almost unbeatable, reputation defeating all his contemporaries including Open winners J.H. Taylor, Harry Vardon and James Braid.

From a very early age, Ben had a wonderful way of teaching both the amateur and professional player. Having a keen eye, he was supreme in diagnosing a player's shortcomings, coupled with a great gift for correcting them, he also instilled confidence in the player. This, along with his brilliant sense of humour, were two of the main characteristics which endeared him to the visiting well-to-do.

Young Ben, like his father, had the talent to be a professional golfer but good golfer that he was - playing for his country three times - he saw his future in teaching the game and making clubs. At the Royal Wimbledon Club where he worked as professional for six years from 1908 he employed six clubmakers making 'brassies', 'cleeks', 'spoons' and drivers along with irons and putters all of which were made and sold by the dozen.

Having served his country during the Great War,

Young Ben and his family returned to North Berwick and the West Links where he joined his father in the family business in the recently acquired clubmaker's premises at the first tee. The business flourished, eventually expanding in 1930 into the factory and foundry buildings located in Forth Street and adjoining High Street retail premises, the latter eventually managed by one of the firm's most colourful characters, George Colley.

Colley was born in Market Place in 1903 and from a young age he and his younger brother were sent 'oot for a cairry' by their mother. 'She would stand doon at the fit of the wynd (steps at the Hope Rooms) wi' her gless' to ensure they went to the green and 'no tae plouter aboot in the burn' George would often regale his customers. Such was the family's need for money, like many other boys at the time, he often carried for members of Society and the business elite. A regular carry was Mrs. Knox D'Arcy, wife of the founder of the Anglo-Persian Oil Company (later BP) for whom he carried for thirteen years and also King Paul of Greece and Princess Ruspoli from Italy. Those and many others were frequent visitors to the High Street shop where George would charm them with stories of the old days and the latest improvements to the Ben Sayers' range.

Sadly, after over thirty years, the shop closed in the mid-sixties when the firm moved to new premises in Dunbar Road - the end on an era for the firm and for golf in North Berwick.

Bernard Sayers' High Street shop where customers from every continent were served and where amateur and professional alike could go and have all their golfing requirements resolved. 1950s

Previous page : Miss Rosie Neuman, a passionate golfer and regular player on the Links at North Berwick. 1920s

Excursions and Day Trips

By the mid-nineteenth century hotel patrons and High Street merchants were offering trips to visitors by carriage to observe the local sites and antiquities. Later fishermen like Thomas Johnston (possibly with financial support from a wealthy local patron) started offering trips by cab to as far as Dunbar, Haddington and Aberlady. Still later, towards the end of that century, newcomers like George Fowler and James Gilbert, seeing potential in the town, started offering tours with their horse-drawn landaus and early motor vehicles.

The Edwardian Era brought improvements in the reliability and performance of motor vehicles with the motorcar and later the chara-banc both proving popular with the wealthy Edwardian traveller. George Fowler took great pride in the appearance of his motor vehicles. In his shop at 64 High Street he had rows of drawers filled with every conceivable size of sponge and chamois leather and other drawers with every imaginable style of spoke brush. The back wall held two racks of tyres with which George's grand-children amused themselves by crawling up the centre. No vehicle was allowed to leave the front of his premises unless both the paint and chromework were gleaming.

Cab Fares			
	mls	s	D
Balgone	3	4	6
Canty Bay	3	4	6
Tantallon Castle	3	4	6
Dirleton Castle	3	4	6
Luchie	3	4	6
Whitekirk	5	7	6
Auldhame & Seacliff	4	6	0
Gullane	5	7	6
Tynningham & Binning Woods		10	0
Drive through Balgone Woods			
Newbyth	6	9	0
Luffness	7	10	6
Aberlady Bay	8	12	0
Gosford	9	14	0
Whittingham	9	15	0
Presmennan Lake	14	21	0
Dunbar	12	16	6
Half-Hour waiting Free			

THOMAS JOHNSTON,

CAB-HIRER AND FISH AGENT,

1 FORTH STREET,

NORTH BERWICK.

Left and Above : Thomas Johnston's business card and list of fares from about 1890. His rates would have been well beyond the means of the ordinary working man - in reality restricted to the well-heeled visitor.

Right : George Fowler awaiting his hire from the Royal Hotel. Fowler was able to offer prospective customers a choice of pony traps, landaus, dog carts and waggonettes for hire. From around 1900 Fowler operated from Market Place with the carriages garaged on the ground floor and his horses stabled on the first floor. Later in 1911, he opened his brand-new premises at 64 High Street, formerly the site of J. Burnet, carriage-hirer.

For locals, the availability of Fowler's and Gilbert's char-a-bancs meant that they too could easily travel out to the country. Local groups and organisations could hire a vehicle and driver for the day - perhaps spending a glorious day down at St. Mary's Loch or elsewhere in the Borders.

By the late 1920s S.M.T.'s buses had established regular routes to North Berwick from the Capital, Dunbar and Haddington providing travellers with an economical form of transport which also enabled them to connect with the bus company's nationwide network. During the summer season this meant that so-called resort towns like North Berwick became even more accessible and within the budget of the majority of working-class families. Eventually bus companies started offering touring holidays lasting a few days or a week – travelling between resorts during the day and stopping over at the next destination the following night.

Left : With the increasing popularity of motor vehicles road maps and guides were produced in ever larger numbers by both the established cartographers and new entrants like motor and petrol companies.

Above : Fowler insisted that no vehicle went out unless its paintwork was gleaming as can be seen above. Notice how the road surface is beautifully reflected in the immaculate paintwork. c1920

Left : On Saturday 27th June 1914, 140 employees of Messrs Flockart & Co. arrived in North Berwick from Edinburgh in a parade of char-a-bancs – similar to the one left. The sight of a convoy of eight or so noisy solid-wheeled mechanical vehicles slowly trundling along the Westgate and High Street would undoubtedly have caused those pedestrians in the vicinity to stop and look on in awe, with nearby children running alongside eager to find out the identity of the passengers.

This grand assemblage of motorcars by the Bass Rock Cycle and Motor Company in about 1910 allows us to imagine the impact the car had on North Berwick. There were other garage proprietors with equally large collections of vehicles. This investment in cars for hire (and there were about 30 of these splendid vehicles available for hire in the town) at a time when cars were, in comparison with today, extremely expensive, highlights the number of wealthy visitors that were coming to the town.

The arrival in North Berwick of such an abundance of motorised transport gave local people the opportunity to venture further afield on their trips out. This photograph, above, of the Abbey Church Choir on a day trip to St Mary's Loch on the 19th June 1913 is a glorious evocation of the Edwardian era - the ladies smartly dressed with large fancy hats and the gentlemen in their three-piece suits with 'Albert' watch chains.

Previous outings by the choir included a trip by train to Loch Lomond (left) when some members took to the water to escape the worst of the stifling heat. Still, it would not have been 'becoming' to have removed one's hat. c1910

By the late 1920s regular buses were running between the Capital and North Berwick and provided a necessary means for many visitors travelling to the town. However by the 1930s the type of vehicle used, double deckers, was causing concern to the Town Council due to the inconvenience and possible risk in the narrow streets of North Berwick. On the 7 July 1931 the Clerk of the Council wrote to the Scottish Motor Traction Company asking them not to send double decker buses to the town and also drew their attention to the Traffic Commissioner report of the inadvisability of such buses. It would appear from the photograph above, taken in the mid-1930s, that S.M.T. reverted back to single-deckers.

Rowing Cobles

The first mention of rowing cobles for hire in North Berwick was recorded in the Town Council minutes in 1886 when Hugh Kirkwood applied for permission to launch his small fleet of rowing boats. He was succeeded by George Stewart and later by members of the various fishing families – Marr, Millar, Pearson, and Thorburn.

During the winter the boats were stored at the old granary above the fishermen's store. Prior to the start of the season the boats were 'sunk' in the sea to allow the timber to absorb water, thereby tightening the joints and making the boats seaworthy and given a lick of fresh white paint. During the season the boats were strung up in the harbour – in the 1930s Percy Pearson's and Ben Millar's boats bobbed about in parallel strings of four or five.

The boats, with the smaller ones taking up to four people and the few larger ones up to six, were always popular - weather permitting - and moored during the day at a narrow movable gangplank.

They provided the opportunity for visiting gentlemen to take the helm to impress their companion with their sea-faring skills – starting off by rowing downwind, oars working beautifully, boat going in a straight line and in the 'right' direction. Problems arose on the way back: against the wind; physical strength waning - if not already gone; travelling backwards instead of forwards and not necessarily in a straight line. If they were lucky they would end up beached across the bay with the 'captain' suffering nothing more than a bit of embarassment and requiring nothing more than the services of a competent local to bring them back.

This is when the barefooted, twelve-year-old local – a Millar, Groom, Pearson, Thorburn, Marr or Dove - came to the rescue. Always on hand, they were ready to help especially when it came to rowing the boats in and out of the harbour. When it came to a rescue, they competently

Previous Page : An early summer's morning preparing to bring ashore the cobles which were moored overnight in the bay. c1900
Right - James 'Daddy' Marr's advert for rowing boats. 1907
Below - A bare-footed Archie Thorburn (centre) ready to help two of George Stewart's young customers - smartly turned out in their starched 'Eton' collars and caps. c1900

56

rowed the boat effortlessly back across the bay into the wind to the little gangplank, saving the passengers and relieving an even more humiliated 'captain' of a few coppers.

It was not always that simple though. Often when the boats had been taken out too far, away from the calm of the bay, they could be caught by a sudden gale coming down the Forth. One such incident happened in June 1919 when two men belonging to the Royal Air Force, based at East Fortune, ended up in the vicinity of the May Island. The lifeboat and crew were launched in the early evening and it was shortly after one o'clock the following morning before the lifeboat returned with the two airmen, fortunately none the worse from their ordeal. Other rowing boats that were caught in the squall were rescued by Ben Millar, Alf Marr and Captain Tom Henderson in their yawls.

Although laid up during the Second War the hiring of rowing boats continued until the sixties when they became non-viable due to lower visitor numbers and the costs of new safety legislation.

Top Left : Neatly moored cobles dancing on the choppy harbour water awaiting more favourable conditions.
Top Right : What a super end to the day! Mooring the boats in the harbour with help from two glamorous visitors.
Bottom Left : Even in the late evening summer sun there was a customer or two for the patient 'coble-master'.
Bottom Right : Archie Thorburn realised that a customer could never be too young - particularly when dressed in a vest, rubber hat and with a strong white belt.
1930s

Beach Huts

Beach huts, or bathing boxes as they were once referred to, were first seen in North Berwick in late Victorian times - often sited individually on either beach following a request for permission to the Burgh Council, mainly by a visitor or his agent. Later, they were mostly available for hire from the Burgh's joiner and cabinetmaker businesses and later still, in 1934, North Berwick Burgh Council decided to proceed the following season with the siting of twelve boxes on the east beach.

Until the early years of the twentieth century, and prior to the West Links being extended seaward, those beach huts on the west bay could be found almost anywhere between the Elcho Slip and Point Garry. At this time, joinery firms Auld, Denholm, Bee and Himsworth erected 50 to 60 boxes between them, exclusive of those owned by private householders. However, due to the concern about the danger to the users of the huts and the hampering of playing golf from the first tee, there followed a meeting between the Council and the North Berwick Club at which it was agreed that boxes should be sited partly to the east and partly to the west of the burn discharging on the beach at the starter's box.

The Council bathing huts, similar in style to those used in Ayr, were located on the east beach opposite the Burgh Clubhouse and were purchased and erected for £15 each. They were available for hire by the season, monthly, fortnightly, weekly, daily, and even for part of a day –

Above : Town Council's Bathing Boxes on the East Bay.
Below : Local joinery firms' adverts from 1920s.

morning, afternoon or evening. Hire charges were set in April 1935, just prior to their first season, at £3 per month for a double to 12s 6d for a single for the week, or part-of-a-day rates ranging from 2s to 1s. Each hut was freshly painted and provided with a seat, mirror and coat pegs. George Johnston, one of the beach cleaners, was put in charge. Unfortunately by mid-June of that year only three had been let and the Council were forced to drop their rates and to improve the amenity of the area. George was required to cut the grass along the shore, keep the beach clean from Yellow Craig eastwards, and discharge other duties as the Burgh Surveyor might determine, for an additional 10/- per week. In addition, to improve the amenity of both beaches the services of an additional man were engaged to clean the remainder of the East Beach and the West Beach, at a wage of £2 per week. Total drawings for the 1935 season amounted to barely £30. All told, after taking account of wages, repairs, maintenance and a fire insurance premium of 5/- per cent per annum, the Council made no profit. Business was not much better the following year even with the Council agreeing a five-year lease with Mrs McKenzie, St Baldred's Tower, on two chalets Nos. 9 and 10 at a rent of £4 each per season. During the War, the Council did not offer their chalets for hire during the season and afterwards only ran them for a few years.

By the early 1920s the beach huts on the West Beach were owned and operated by the Westgate firm of William Auld & Son. In late spring, the beach above the high water mark in front of the West Links' starter's box, was cleared by Willie Auld and his team of workers in preparation for the delivery of the huts. The huts were stored over winter on the ground floor of the old granary building in Harbour Terrace. Until the early part of the twentieth century they were delivered to the beach by horse and cart and later on Bert Young's flat-bed lorry. Each of the

For some families their holiday by the beach was the only time in the year they may have spent together and was an opportunity to let their hair down - except for Grandad who was never without his jacket, tie and 'bunnet'. 1930s

For Auld's joiners, with clean white shirts and ties, a brief moment to relax for the camera before starting to erect the last of the huts for the season. Later, once the season got under way the joiners would furnish each hut with deck chairs and wind-breaks as required by the summer residents. c1929

36 huts, freshly painted, 18 in green and 18 in yellow livery, were bedded down on a couple of bricks and there they would sit happily all summer under their own weight.

Invariably, the huts were let to the same tenants each year, mostly by the season, but occasionally by the month, with No. 5 retained for the Auld family's own use. The tenants would post their requirements for deck chairs and windbreaks to Auld's shop in the Westgate and it was from there that Sandy Millar would manhandle the tenant's requirements down to the respective hut by hand-barrow. The ambience along this part of the beach with the huts, was of a coastal village where everyone knew their neighbours: catching up on news, preparing meals on their primus stove, and awaiting fathers' return from work in the city.

The early seventies saw the demise of the beach huts due to more people travelling to the Spanish Costas, vandalism, and the cost of renting the beach from the Council. Huts were put up for sale at £25 each with the majority sold to previous tenants from the west coast, many eager to relocate them in their own garden.

Above and Page opposite : Summer scenes of contentment along the West Bay. 1930s
Right : A happy trio ready for some beach excavation with their buckets and spades. 1971

Postcards

The custom of sending postcards started towards the end of the Victorian era when the Post Office introduced a plain pre-stamped card for sale – with space for an address on one side and a brief note on the other. From about 1900, the Post Office first allowed postcards, published by others, to be sent by post with a halfpenny stamp. Picture postcards soon followed, although since one side was still retained for the address and nothing else, it meant that with the picture on the other side there was often little room for the message. In 1902 the Post Office changed its rules and allowed pictures to appear on the front of postcards with the address and message on the 'divided back' similar to the cards which have been sent by millions of holiday-makers since.

In North Berwick, like all summer resorts, postcards were very popular. As well as cards from the popular publishers like 'Valentine', 'Reliable' and 'Tuck's', many postcards were commissioned by local High Street retailers like newsagents, Bertram and Hill, Henderson's, Green's and Danks'. Other cards were manufactured in-house with Thomas Wilson's High Street shop, 'The White House', being one of the main producers. The shop was a tourist haven selling a cornucopia of tourist gifts ranging from large photographic prints to 'Goss' chinaware. Another local, Reginald Phillimore, started printing, publishing and distributing nationwide postcards based on his own artwork. Others in the town, including photographers James Balmain and George Day and newsagent Tom Danks, licensed their own photographs to the main publishers with Dundee-based 'Valentine' being one of the main buyers.

Left : This romantic image with its reference to 'Canty Bay' has been reproduced especially for the local market. Unfortunately for our four-legged friend his master has directed his attention elsewhere.

Below : Old postcards preserve historical scenes from a past age. This harbour scene from the 1920s was taken prior to railings being erected to prevent vehicles accidently ending up in the harbour. This was the case in 1930 when a lady engaged the wrong gear and resulted in her drowning after her car 'took-off' into the harbour at high water.

Above : Many cards reproduced paintings by local artists. This image shows a fisherman's cottage on land that is now between Melbourne Place and Melbourne Road. A fisherman's wife can be seen at the cottage door admiring her beautiful, colourful garden.

On the Cliffs at Canty Bay.

NORTH BERWICK, HARBOUR & QUALITY STREET

The multiview card has always been popular - perhaps because it allows the buyer to purchase a number of views for the price of one.

VALENTINE'S SNAPSHOTS
12 REAL PHOTOGRAPHS FOR YOUR ALBUM 1/-
NORTH BERWICK
TITLES ON THE REVERSE SIDE OF THE PHOTOS
PRINTED IN GT BRITAIN

Examples of novelty fold-out cards from the 1930s with Valentine's mini-pack of 'real photographs', above, and Tuck's souvenir 'Letterview', right. Both versions allowed the sender, to indulge the lucky recipient, with a bounty of images from their resort of choice.

This postcard posted in 1911 with a touch of tartan and heather gives a 'real' feel of Scotland and was a popular way of encouraging foreign tourists to buy a postcard.

During the Edwardian period there were numerous uplifts of post each working day enabling a sender to communicate with the recipient speedily and efficiently. This card was uplifted at 6.15pm with the message telling the recipient to expect the sender on the 10.00am train the following day.

63

Swimming Costumes

Since the earliest days of taking to the sea for pleasure, swimming costume fashions have changed dramatically – from serge swimming dresses in the Victorian Era to skimpy bikinis and trunks today. Victorian outfits, revealed when one exited the bathing machine, look totally impractical for swimming to our eyes and likely to require the assistance of one or two fully-dressed servants. Today costumes for competition swimmers are made from materials that replicate sharkskin – to help the swimmer slip through the water with minimal effort.

In between these two periods swimming costumes have steadily become more revealing and more practical, particularly with the use of man-made fabrics. There was also a period in the first half of last century when making costumes for children and grandchildren was quite popular - either knitted or sewn-up in fashionable fabric. Unfortunately many of the costumes were anything but practical with the wearer of a knitted one-piece often, when leaving the water, caught fighting back the tears while rushing for the changing cubicle as the crotch of the costume sagged below the knees.

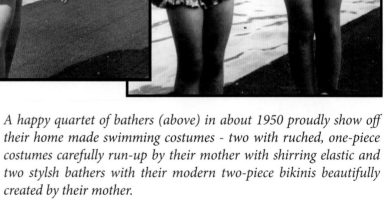

A happy quartet of bathers (above) in about 1950 proudly show off their home made swimming costumes - two with ruched, one-piece costumes carefully run-up by their mother with shirring elastic and two stylsh bathers with their modern two-piece bikinis beautifully created by their mother.

Unfortunately this little Edwardian bather (left) looks somewhat glum standing all alone on Broadsands in an eye-catching one-piece swimming costume with its complementary rubber hat. Perhaps a friend in an equally dazzling costume will come along in a minute?

On the 7th July 1936 the Pondmaster, Mr James McCracken, wrote to the Town Council regarding his concerns about enforcing one of the byelaws of the swimming pond namely - 'A person above the age of eight years of age, resorting to the swimming pond and while using the same, must wear a bathing costume from neck to knee.' However with the use of trunks and topless swimsuits throughout the country, he was finding it increasingly difficult to enforce the regulation at North Berwick Swimming Pond. Unfortunately for Mr McCracken, the Council resolved that the regulation, as defined by the byelaws, should be adhered to. Clearly the groups of bathers above would have a problem adhering to the said byelaw if they choose to swim in the pond in their shorter, more revealing costumes and would require Mr McCracken to turn a blind eye.

North Berwick Swimming Pond

- the formation of a Swimming Club, the opening of the Swimming Pond and its early years

Early in the second half of the nineteenth century there was a growing awareness of the need to prevent the loss of life through drowning. In 1868 Dr MacBean suggested to the Town Council the propriety of encouraging the formation of a swimming club in the town with a view to lessening the risks from drowning. Increasingly there was the likelihood of a death by drowning in one of the bays over the summer season, due to the increasingly popular pastime of bathing. Locally, in 1889, monies raised by subscription paid for buoys and ropes to be located in each bay and paid the expenses of a man and boat to watch over the bathers – at least as well as one man could - for the season. Unfortunately there were insufficient monies available to cover a man's expenses for future years. Nationally the benefits of outdoors bathing were being recognised with the eighteen-nineties seeing an increasing number of public bathing ponds being opened. In 1888 Mr Galloway, owner of the steamboats, suggested that salt-water baths be created at the east end of the harbour using part of the 'flushing pond'.

Finally in 1896, a swimming club, consisting of junior and senior sections, was formally instituted as the North Berwick Swimming Club and Humane Society. Initiated by Sir Walter Hamilton Dalrymple the club was formalised at a well-attended public meeting in the Forester's Hall with Sir Walter appointed Honorary President and Dr Frank Crombie, President. It was intimated at the meeting

the need for 'lads to learn the useful art of swimming' if not through the Board schools at least as early as possible with the suggestion that the most suitable place to learn was the 'Leithies.'

The following year, as part of the town's Diamond Jubilee celebrations, the club held a grand aquatic gala in the harbour. Probably the first aquatic gala held in the town, the event featured swimming exhibitions by champions from Edinburgh, a rescue demonstration

Part of the 'Flushing Pond' on the east side of the harbour. c1880

Above : 'Grand Aquatic Gala' held during the celebrations for Queen Victoria's Diamond Jubilee 1897
Left : Advert from the Haddingtonshire Courier 6 August 1897.

by the Western S.C., and various open events. The successful event was held on the 14th August and was attended by crowds of residents and visitors.

In August 1899, following a couple of years of increasing patronage, the club forwarded a proposal to the Town Council proposing the erection of a safety swimming pond, for instruction in the art of swimming, along with suitable bathing accommodation. The proposed site was to the east of the harbour on what had been a domestic rubbish and sewerage site – thankfully emptied by the tide twice daily - and was duly approved by the Council, following Provost MacIntyre's explanation of what such an acquisition's importance would be to the town. Following the approval, a committee was appointed to carry out the work in the terms of the plans submitted, to raise such funds as required to carry out the work and do what was necessary to promote its use. It was also felt that the pond should ultimately pass to the Town Council, as representatives of the community, though not

before the scheme was entirely free from debt.

A circular was issued in the name of the Provost and given to both residents and visitors explaining the scheme and inviting subscriptions. The expected sum was £250 and if raised it was hoped that work would start at an early date. The following month the Committee placed an article in the Haddingtonshire Courier thanking all the subscribers for their generous support and confirmed that £256 7 shillings had been raised and intimating, however, that further donations would be necessary for the satisfactory completion of the scheme.

Work started almost immediately with the appointment of the architectural practice of Belfrage and Carfrae, an Edinburgh firm of civil engineers. Stone was blasted and hewn from the rocks, progressively deeper towards the harbour end - which was to be separated from the pond by a robust Law-stone wall. Concrete was poured over the surface to provide a shallow 'Vee' providing a safe,

Early days of the pond with its rudimentary slide and diving steps and greasy pole for the brave. c1905

gentle swimming area and a sloping terrace for spectators. Around the perimeter, benches were positioned to allow onlookers to enjoy the aquatic frolicking and antics and space was also allowed for that most respectable of Edwardian pursuits, promenading. In the north corner, a structure made entirely from wood was provided for changing. Later, to be known locally as 'The Ark', the building provided cover but precious little shelter from the elements and if a bather was unfortunate enough to stand on the wooden floor where a knot had loosened and fallen out there was sure to be a mighty draft up the legs. By the end of the following summer, the pond, which measured 170 feet by 125 feet, was ready for use. On the 16th September 1900, the new safety-swimming pond was opened by the Right Honourable the Lord Justice-General in the presence of nearly 3000 residents and visitors. The pond had cost £527 of which £380 had been subscribed. The proceedings of the day were expected to reduce the deficit further through the generosity of the paying attendees as barricades had been erected at the bottom of Victoria Road ensuring that all those passing to watch the opening spectacle were charged for access.

During the opening regatta the audience was shown exhibitions of graceful diving and impressive displays of artistic and fast swimming. There followed a series of handicap races between Wynman Swimming Club from Edinburgh and local representatives as well as a number of sailing and rowing races in the open sea, and finally an exhibition of water polo between North Berwick and Wynman which the home team won by two goals to nil. Later, in the Imperial Hotel, where tea was served, Dr Frank Crombie gave a hearty vote of thanks to the Edinburgh Club.

During the early years, the Pond Committee was anxious to clear the outstanding debt and held a number of successful fundraising events – evening concerts, dances, fancy dress cycle parades and aquatic galas. By 1906, following the final gala of the year at which a profit of £36 was realised, the committee was in a position to hand over the pond to the Town Council. In accepting the pond on behalf of the community, the Council recognised in their minutes 'the committee's success in not only forming the pond but also greatly improving the locality by their operations.' The total cost had been about £800 which included further changing boxes, a box for the pond-master, a slide and diving apparatus.

Over the next thirty or so years, the pond was continually upgraded and improved. It was enlarged and new diving boards installed – the original were rather crude and prone to sway in high winds - and new changing cubicles built along the west and north with some having electric heaters installed in 1935 for which a bather was charged an extra 1d.

Possibly the only surviving photograph of the opening regatta.

69

Fancy Dress Cycle Parades

Fancy dress cycle parades became very popular during the Edwardian Period and provided the opportunity to raise funds for a chosen good cause. The bikes were highly decorated with crepe paper, ribbon, flags, bunting and almost any other thing imaginable. The owner, and it was mostly girls who took part in the event, dressed in a complementary outfit to match the theme of the bike. Plans for an outfit started weeks before the big day and would involve consulting friends and relatives for its approval, begging from shops and other outlets for suitable material scraps to construct the mobile display, and finally enlisting mother's and neighbours' help to bring it altogether.

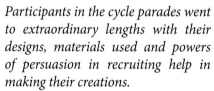

Participants in the cycle parades went to extraordinary lengths with their designs, materials used and powers of persuasion in recruiting help in making their creations.

The parade on Wednesday evening the 16th August 1905 was typical of a fancy dress cycle parade. The cyclists assembled that evening at the new esplanade and then, headed by the North Berwick Pipe Band, rode in procession through the town. Visitors and residents co-operated to make the display as dazzling and colourful as possible with many dressed in magnificent costumes, some in humorous character and others dressed as scary, grotesque monsters. Some dressed as characters

Miss Margaret (Maud) Neill, 'Little Red Riding Hood', aged 7, ready to take part in the cycle parade on the 16th August 1905 to raise funds for the swimming pond. Her outfit and crepe paper decorations were made by the daughters of Mr Robertson, the blacksmith, who lived next door in Market Place. Maud won second prize in the under 14 category.

from story books, while others dressed as people from foreign lands and some as people at work, with a Chinaman, kitchen-maid, and Indian chief amongst the characters. Later, after the first parade, the competitors took part in a lantern precession around the principal streets when the effect of the costumes was even more striking. In total about £30 was collected in tins for the swimming pond fund. And still later, even more money was collected when a dance was held in the Forester's Hall during which about 80 couples, mostly in fancy dress, took to the floor before a large number of spectators.

Fancy dress cycle parades, often organised by the Bass Rock Cycle Club, continued in popularity into the 1920s when they became part of general fancy dress gala days which were also becoming popular and involved all modes of transport. During their heyday, participants raised valuable funds for the likes of the Reading and Recreation Club, a miniature rifle range for the North Berwick branch of the British Legion, and for the Edinburgh Royal Infirmary.

Pierrots, witches, kitchen produce, cleaning products, the four seasons, were just a few of the creations thought up by the entrants. Many of the outfits were recycled and reused at future events - sometimes by succeeding generations.

Esplanade Entertainers

It was in 1896 when the Town Council started receiving requests for permission to provide entertainment at the harbour. Mr Samual Evans, a Hobby Horse Proprietor from Portobello, applied unsuccessfully in that year and, along with a growing number of other performers, he applied in each of the following years for a lease to provide entertainment at the harbour. Finally from 1905, permission for *al fresco* entertainment to the growing number of summer visitors was granted by the Council on the harbour esplanade. The ground at the harbour, formerly a piece of waste ground had been laid with concrete the previous year. A lease for the first 'summer season' was issued to Lesley Lynn to commence first June at £1 per week. Unfortunately the rental monies were not forthcoming and it was only with some reluctance that the site was let again the following year. Again the let was not without its problems which included performers touting for donations from swimming pond spectators on the Platcock Rocks and with performances continuing late into the night.

Eventually a formal lease was drawn up for entertainers to sign compelling the lessee to provide at least six artists and that they be smartly and suitable attired, performances to be select and refined; that he keep good order; provide his own suitable stage - ensuring it was smartly painted and came with all accessories and seating; performances to end no later than 9.55pm; and no collections to be made from the Platcock Rocks during performances.

Over the coming years visitors grew to expect to see entertainers at the harbour esplanade. Groups such as 'Erick's Entertainers' and 'Joe Anderson's Open-Air Entertainers' were among the most popular with the large crowds that gathered twice daily to see their shows. The artists performed from a small 'tented' stage erected specifically for their use on the harbour esplanade. Seating cost 3d with the price never changing over the twenty-five years or so that performers enthralled their audiences on the esplanade. However most spectators stood outside the seating area escaping charge but not the persistence of the collectors jangling their metal buckets. By the early 1930s the popularity of the pierrot shows on the esplanade was starting to wane being replaced with indoor performances in the Oddfellows' Hall and later by more up-to-date seaside entertainment – stage shows provided in the new Pavilion.

Above : A small crowd of Edwardian spectators gather round the rather rudimentary stage come changing-room affair to hear the latest popular tunes from the troupe of five artists - four men and one lady. The audience are likely to be mainly visitors to the town - possibly staying in houses they have taken for the fortnight or month. The ladies are dressed in full length dresses, many of which are still black, reminiscent of the days of mourning during the Victorian period, but a few are white or of a light colour more favoured during the reign of Edward VII. The men are all dressed in dark-coloured suits and hats with many being straw boaters. c1908

Previous Page : 'Erick's Entertainers' playing to a large assemblage of onlookers - most of whom choose to forgo the 3d 'entrance' charge by standing on the periphery. One lady is dressed in a maid's uniform - possibly assisting her employer 'the Lady of the House' with the pram? Those facing away from the pierrots are watching bathers in the pool seated on the new benches positioned for their use by the Burgh Council in about 1910. The building on the right is part of what was the Council's old stables, newly extended and upgraded to provide shelter during a summer shower. c1912

Photo by J. Dickson, North Berwick]   LYNN AND ALLAN'S ENTERTAINERS, NORTH BERWICK AND DUNBAR.

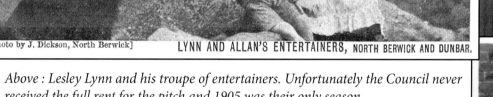

Above : Lesley Lynn and his troupe of entertainers. Unfortunately the Council never received the full rent for the pitch and 1905 was their only season.

Top Right : Fred Erick (standing left with his wife, Lois Audrey seated) and his entertainers arrived in North Berwick for the 1910 season and with a few omissions during the Great War, performed each season until 1920. During their tenure not everything ran smoothly. During their second season Harry Newton, the pianist, had a narrow escape while practising swimming at the pond. On going down the chute he became somewhat excited - no doubt realising he was in the deep-end and unable to swim. Fortunately, Mr Hope, the swimming master swam to his assistance, and promptly brought him to safety. The Council, despite selling Erick the chairs from the swimming pond for a very reasonable 1/6, on condition that they were available for each gala, struggled at times during his tennacy to obtain the full amout due in rent.

Bottom Right : Joe Anderson's entertainers took over the tenancy at the Harbour Esplanade from Erick in 1921 and continued to perform there each season until the Pavilion opened. Thereafter, his troupe performed for a couple of seasons in the Oddfellows' Hall.

"Joe Anderson's Entertainers, North Berwick 1932."

75

Pond-masters

From the very beginning the responsibility for the smooth running of the swimming pond was that of the pond-master, who having been appointed by the Town Council, had to conform to all its instructions and that of its Entertainments Committee and convener. Required to live in the town, the pond-master was expected to take an interest in the local swimming club and while at the pond, exercise general supervision over all the bathers and ensure that the bye-laws governing the pond were adhered to.

Amongst his other duties, the details of which changed over the years, the pond-master also had the responsibility for cleaning the pond and all property associated with it, including bathing cubicles although he could request a cleaning assistant on application to the Burgh Surveyor. When the pond water was changed, he was required to seek the supervision of the Burgh Engineer (later surveyor) when pumping fresh water into the pond.

Also included in the pond-master's duties, was informing the Council when equipment required replacing, where a replacement might be sourced and the likely cost. Arranging suitable entertainers for the summer galas was also within his remit along with reporting their likely fee to the Council.

The pond-master also carried out the duties of swimming master, giving lessons in swimming, diving and natation for which he was entitled to charge such fees as he might consider reasonable. Also the pond-master was permitted to give exhibitions connected with swimming and diving no more than once a fortnight and be allowed to take collections. The hiring of costumes was also permitted but no garment could be sold. He was also allowed to employ an assistant at his own expense.

Mr McCracken in the children's pond (right) dressed in his bodywaders, teaching a mother to swim while her daughter looks on. She looks a little uncomfortable as McCracken encourages her while he keeps her head out the water with his hand under her chin. His two assistants stand by on the boom with their cane poles ready to give assistance to anyone who gets into difficulty. c1931

A TOUCH OF THE HOUDINIS

NORTH BERWICK swimming pool galas were exciting affairs if this Balmain photograph is anything to go by. Taken in August 1928 it shows Freddie Lemmon performing the Monte Cristo Sack Dive. Mr Lemmon was tied in a sack and then pushed from the high diving board by pondmaster James McCracken. To heighten the drama Mr Lemmon remained submerged for over a minute before surfacing at another part of the pool to gasps of 'oohs' and 'ahhs' from the spectators thronging the poolside.

Above Left : Freddie Lemmon (centre) and his two assistants, always immaculately turned out, pose for the photographer before starting another day's instruction and supervision. c1930

Above Right : This happy little bather, Freddie Lemmon's daughter, dressed in her woollen bathing costume, has been snapped by Mr Balmain, the photographer, enjoying a cup of Bovril made by her mother in the little kiosk, after a bracing swim in the unheated pond. c1930

Top Right : Press cutting from 1928.

Bottom Right : Freddie Lemmon's card showing his terms of engagement. The cost of lessons - 8/6d for a single lesson and three guineas for a series of eight - would have been beyond the reach of working class bathers. Fortunately, for local school children, free swimming lessons were introduced in 1913 under the tutelage of the pond-master, Mr Hope.

NORTH BERWICK SWIMMING POND	SEASON 1956
	TERMS FOR TUITION
	Course of Eight Individual Lessons in Swimming or Diving - £3 3 0
Pondmaster and Principal Teacher FRED. W. LEMMON, R.L.S.S. and Diploma.	Single Lesson - - - - - - 0 8 6
	Duration of Lesson approximately 15 minutes
Assistants Mr. I. W. LEMMON Mr. A. INGOLDSBY Mr. A. WOOD	CLASS INSTRUCTION IN CRAWL, BACK CRAWL AND GENERAL WATERMANSHIP
	PRIVATE SCHOOLS BY ARRANGEMENT

From 1921, the pond-master was entitled to sell hot drinks - Cocoa and Bovril - with invariably the pond-master's wife taking responsibility for the selling of the so-called 'shivery-bites', perhaps with sugar stars or iced gems – packets of little biscuits topped with icing - or Brodie's pies, fresh daily, and all sold from a small kiosk.

Up until 1920 there were three main pond-masters. Mr. Hope was employed both before and after the Great War and when he was called up to go to the Front to serve his country, the position became the responsibility of a woman. Firstly Miss Alison Wilkie from Edinburgh, who was the only applicant for the position in 1916 and became the first swimming-mistress. Due to the Council's concern for safety – there being, unusually a female pond-mistress - the Clerk arranged for a 'swimming dress' for Miss Wilkie, so that in the event of an emergency she should be ready to enter the water. Unfortunately the Council minutes hold no details of the dress's style or design. However Miss Wilkie was well thought of by her employers and in recognition of her success in running the pond and galas was presented with a gift of two guineas on the event of her marriage. For the following year a Miss Baillie was appointed with a salary of 30 shillings - 10/- more than her predecessor.

From 1920 through until the pond closed in 1995, there were six main pond-masters – Jim McCracken always referred to as 'Mr McCracken', Freddie Lemmon, Drew Kennedy, Eric Smith, Sandy Jenson and Shona McDonald.

Below left : Drew Kennedy, playing the bamboo pole air-guitar and (top left) giving an exhibition of acrobatics. 1960s

Below right : Eric Smith and his wife, Evelyn, giving a diving exhibition during an afternoon gala. c1966

Top right : Sandy Jenson encouraging six cold, swimming pupils to take the plunge. c1977

Beach Parties

A group photograph taken on the beach can give a fascinating insight into changes in dress and appearance over the years, particularly in the first half of the twentieth century. Early photographs from that period often show grandparents still in Victorian attire – black and subdued colours with women in full-length dresses and gentlemen in three-piece suits. Later, towards the middle of the twentieth century, younger generations appear in more revealing summerwear.

Below Left : Taken towards the end of the Victorian era, this family portrait shows a mother and her three sons posed for the photographer. None look comfortable, yet they know it is something they must endure - possibly the photograph is to send to the lady's husband who may be fighting in some distant war.

Below Centre : A group taken in August 1935. Granny, with her Edwardian hat and knitting, with her son and his family and friends. The young ladies' clothes are made from cooler fabrics in light colours more appropriate for the time of year. Father is still dressed relatively formally in his suit, although his shoes are more appropriate for the occasion. However the children's nurse is still required to dress in full uniform.

Above : A cheerful family occasion at Point Garry with the younger generations relaxed and comfortable posing for the photograph. Granny, with her large hat and dark long skirt, and grandfather, in his dark three-piece suit and shirt with starched collar, look somewhat more formal.

Below : A happy family group taken in the 1950s without a single item of dark clothing - the ladies in colourful floral dresses and the gents in open collared shirt or topless. And the young children à la mode in swimming costumes - the boys in trunks and the girls in ruched one-pieces.

Ice-cream

Although a version of ice cream was made by the Ancient Persians and later the Romans, it was not until the Victorians and the availability of refrigeration that it became available to the masses. Regular requests to North Berwick Town Council for permission to supply refreshments were being received as early as 1898 – all of which were refused. It was not until the 1920s when the Council relented and let four stances on Harbour Terrace for the sale of ice cream and other refreshments – much to the disapproval of George Thomson, tenant of the L.B. Café (subsequently Capaldi's and later Mario's). Tenancies for the ice-cream stances were sold annually for a seasonal rent of about ten guineas. Regular takers in the 1920s and thirties were Luca Scappaticcio and various members of the Di Rollo family.

Two more happy customers (above) enjoy their penny cornets bought from Luca's stance on Harbour Terrace in 1932. The Terrace (left) was a busy throughfare in summer with visitors and locals alike as they made their way to and from the swimming pond. It was popular with ice-cream vendors - including Luca Scappaticcio and Thomas di Rollo - enticing prospective customers with their frozen confections. 1927

SELLING ICE-CREAM AFTER HOURS – Yesterday, in Haddington Sheriff Court Erminto Valerio, ice-cream dealer, pleaded guilty to having on Saturday, 24th July, in his shop in North Berwick's High Street, sold ice-cream after 9p.m., contrary to the Early Closing Shops Order. The accused said he sold other refreshments for which he could keep open after 9p.m. On this occasion, his wife was very busy, and did not know the hour, as they had no clock in the shop. Sheriff MacLeod imposed a fine of £1.

Haddingtonshire Courier 13 August 1920

In 1930 the arrival of Mr Togneri's ice-cream van at Scoughall Caravan Park was always popular and brought out wide smiles on his happy customers' faces - and some rather well-balanced headwear!

After a hard day at the yachting pond there was nothing better than a wafer basket and ice-cream and don't our bare-footed beach-revellers look as if they are enjoying them? 1950s

S. LUCA

FOR ICE CREAM MADE WITH
FRESH MILK AND DOUBLE CREAM

STANCES AT NORTH BERWICK

37-39 HIGH STREET : MUSSELBURGH

AND

34 QUALITY STREET : NORTH BERWICK

Telephone: MUSselburgh 2237   Telephone: 3189

S Luca, the Musselburgh ice cream manufacturer, opened a cafe in Quality Street, North Berwick in the 1960s. Always popular, it was a great place for teenagers to hang out with friends - sharing a hot-orange on a wet summer's day.

North Berwick Yacht Club

Following months of talk culminating in a specially convened meeting of small boat owners in the Oddfellow's Hall in June 1901, the North Berwick Yacht Club was formed. Captain Thomas Henderson was appointed first Commodore along with a committee comprising mainly of local businessmen. Their prime aim was to organise fortnightly races throughout the summer months and, in August of the same year, the club planned to hold its first regatta which was open to craft from the whole Firth of Forth. Before club membership was issued, prospective entrants were required to pass an exam set by Master Mariner Henderson proving their sailing competence.

Over the course of the season, race competitors competed for a silver trophy, the Henderson Cup generously presented by the popular commodore, collecting points awarded to the first three in each race.

Above : The Mayflower (right) takes an early lead from Dragon (front right) and Paragon (front left). c1910

Left : Some members of North Berwick Yacht Club with their 1919 champion James Henderson (seated with hat and tie) with the Henderson Trophy in the foreground. Amongst those present are Ben Millar, James 'Daddy' Marr, Carl Henderson, and James Henderson jnr.

The races, with up to a dozen yachts competing, sailed under time handicaps over a course of about six miles – round Fidra and the Craig and back to the harbour. Boats such as Henderson's 'Dragon', Liston Blyth's 'Eos', Wightman's 'Paragon', Nelson's 'Mayflower', Smith's 'Tern', Denholm's 'Mary', Richardson's 'Fiona', Hutchison's 'Sunbeam' and 'Daddy' Marr's 'Cymba' were regularly turned out for the Thursday and Saturday afternoon races.

During the Great War pleasure sailing was suspended but by 1919 competition amongst the local sailing fraternity had recommenced. Unfortunately there was not the same level of competition and interest in the club started to peter out and when Captain Henderson died in 1929 the club was wound-up.

North Berwick Yacht Club – North Berwick Yacht Club held their first race for the Commodore's Cup when nine yachts competed. The winner was Mr. James Henderson's Dragon. Baillie Nelson's Mayflower won second prize and Thomas Hutchison's Sunbeam third.
Haddingtonshire Courier 24 June 1914

Below : Climax to a race with the competitors returning to the West Bay. c1910
Below Right : The 1914 Commodore's Trophy made by Sheffield silversmiths, Walker & Hall.

Town Council Guide Books

NORTH BERWICK

Jas. C. H. Balmain   Copyright
No. Berwick

THE OFFICIAL PUBLICATION OF
THE CORPORATION

THE GUIDE BOOK – The Town Council have this season issued a new and up-to-date edition of the Guide Book of the town. The information within its pages cannot fail to be of interest to visitors and the various views are exceedingly good - these including two pictures of Whitekirk Church, the one after a snowstorm, and the other showing the building in its devastated state. Two thousand copies are being issued this season, 500 of which have been sent to Manchester alone, while the booklet can also be found at many of the railway stations. From day to day, the Town Clerk is receiving many enquiries from prospective visitors from all parts, including one from France this week.

Haddingtonshire Courier 5 June 1914

*Some of the many guides published by North Berwick Town Council
- clockwise from top right 1973, 1959, 1963,1950s, 1940s and 1920s*

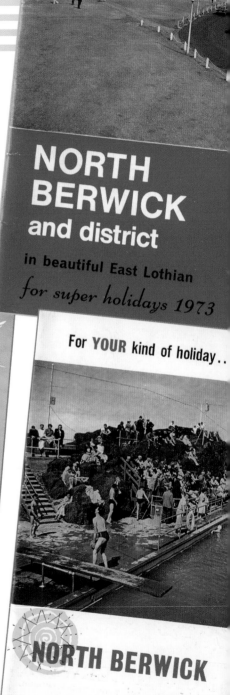

NORTH BERWICK and district

in beautiful East Lothian

for super holidays 1973

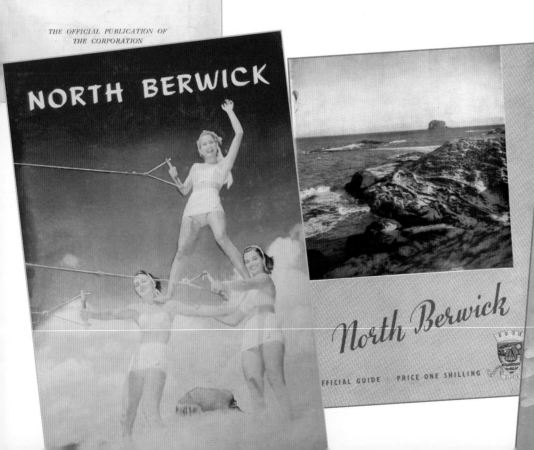

NORTH BERWICK

North Berwick

OFFICIAL GUIDE · PRICE ONE SHILLING

North BERWICK

VICTORIAE · MERCES · GLORIA

The Scottish Holiday Resort

OFFICIAL GUIDE

For YOUR kind of holiday..

NORTH BERWICK

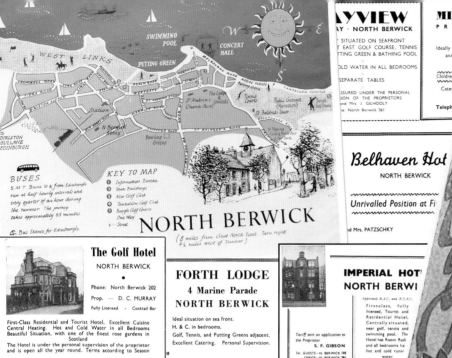

NORTH BERWICK

(8 miles from Great North Road. Turn right 4½ miles west of Dunbar)

KEY TO MAP
1. Information Bureau
2. Town Buildings
3. New Golf Club
4. Tantallon Golf Club
5. Burgh Golf Course
— One Way
← → Street

BUSES
S M T Buses to & from Edinburgh run at half-hourly intervals and every quarter of an hour during the summer. The journey takes approximately 65 minutes.

Bus Stance for Edinburgh

BAYVIEW
BAY · NORTH BERWICK

SITUATED ON SEAFRONT
ST EAST GOLF COURSE, TENNIS
TTING GREEN & BATHING POOL

OLD WATER IN ALL BEDROOMS

SEPARATE TABLES

SSURED UNDER THE PERSONAL
ION OF THE PROPRIETORS

Phone: North Berwick 361

MILSEY HOUSE
PRIVATE HOTEL
TANTALLON TERRACE

Ideally situated on Sea Front, adjacent to Burgh Golf
and convenient to Tennis Courts and Putting Green

Every Home Comfort Assured

Children Welcome   Open all Year   Terms

Catering and Management under Personal Supervision
of Proprietors

Telephone - 311   Mr. and Mrs. T. P.

CAIRNSMORE
PRIVATE HOTEL
MARINE PARADE

H. & C. IN
ALL ROOMS

Beautifully situated in East
outlook to Bass Rock and
Sandy beach in front. B
House. Two minutes
Tennis, Putting. Highly re
for excellent cooking a
Home baking a specia

Terms on application from
Mr. and Mrs. HACKMAN

ELPHINSTONE HOTEL
WEST BAY

★ H. and C. in all Bedrooms
★ Excellent and varied cuisine
★ Garage and Parking on Premises
★ Gas Fires in most Bedrooms

OPEN

COLUMBA PRIVATE HOTEL
MARINE PARADE

This hotel is situated in
its own grounds on the
sea front commanding
an excellent view of the
Firth of Forth. Adjoin-
ing Tennis Courts and
Putting Greens and near
Golf Course and Swim-
ming Pool. H. & C. in
all bedrooms. Washing
and Ironing facilities.
Special terms for
Children.

Telegrams:
"Columba" North Berwick

Preps: Mr. & Mrs. H. L. CLARK

NDHURST
MELBOURNE ROAD

☆ On Sea Front
☆ Near Swimming Pool, Tennis,
   Putting, Golf, etc.
☆ Home Baking
☆ Children Welcome
☆ Open all year round
☆ Terms on application

Proprietrix: Mrs. M. G.

Bramerton Hotel (FULLY LICENSED)
DIRLETON AVENUE   NORTH BERWICK

Pleasantly situated in own grounds, on main bus
route. Two minutes from Golf Links, Beach and
Railway Station. Well-cooked, tastefully-served
Meals. Comfortably furnished Rooms with hot
and cold water in Bedrooms.
Brochure and Terms on request.
Open throughout the year.
Bus Parties catered for.

RESTAURANT
AND BAR OPEN TO
NON-RESIDENTS

Phone: NORTH BERWICK 228

— personal supervision of the Proprietor, Mrs. M. F. Davidson

---

Belhaven Hotel
NORTH BERWICK

Unrivalled Position at Fi

nd Mrs. PATZSCHKY

The Golf Hotel
NORTH BERWICK

Phone: North Berwick 202
Prop.: D. C. MURRAY
Fully Licensed • Cocktail Bar

First-Class Residential and Tourist Hotel. Excellent Cuisine
Central Heating. Hot and Cold Water in all Bedrooms
Beautiful Situation, with one of the finest rose gardens in
Scotland
The Hotel is under the personal supervision of the proprietor
and is open all the year round. Terms according to Season

FORTH LODGE
4 Marine Parade
NORTH BERWICK

Ideal situation on sea front.
H. & C. in bedrooms.
Golf, Tennis, and Putting Greens adjacent.
Excellent Catering. Personal Supervision.

Tariff sent on application to
the Proprietor
S. F. GIBSON

Tel: GUESTS—N. BERWICK 105
OFFICE—N. BERWICK 361

IMPERIAL HOTEL
NORTH BERWICK

Appointed R.A.C. and R.S.A.C.

First-class, fully
licensed, Tourist and
Residential Hotel,
Centrally situated,
near golf, tennis and
swimming pool. The
Hotel has Room Radi
and all bedrooms ha
hot and cold runni
water

Mr. & Mrs. J. E. PEND

THE COUNTY HOTEL
NORTH BERWICK

FULLY LICENSED

Within 5 minutes' walk of Swimming Pool,
Golf, Tennis, Bowling and Putting Green.
Good Food—Good Beds—Dining Room—
Cocktail Bar and Lounge open to non-
residents.

CASTLE HOTEL
DIRLETON

In Scotland's loveliest village between Gullane

'ALDERSYDE'
PRIVATE HOTEL
DIRLETON AVENUE

Under Personal Supervision of
Proprietrix: Miss E. Reid
Telephone, North Berwick 341

Situated on bus route and within a few minutes of West Links
Golf Course, Station, Beach, Putting Greens etc.
Patrons are assured of every comfort and attention.

BRENTWOOD HOTEL
MARMION ROAD - NORTH BERWICK

Proprietor:
R. KING

Personal
Supervision

Phone 124

SITUATED NEAR STATION, BOWLING GREENS AND BEACH

FORTH
Guest House
5 MARINE PARADE
NORTH BERWICK

View from Lounge Window

Ideally situated on Sea Front (sandy beach). Adjacent to Putting
Greens and Tennis Courts. Near Golf Course and Bathing Pool

HIGHLY RECOMMENDED   SEPARATE TABLES
H. and C. IN BEDROOMS   CENTRAL HEATING

Proprietors: Mr. and Mrs. E. M. Kirkwood   Telephone: North Berwick 191

Eastfield Hotel
1 Marine Parade
North Berwick

Beautifully situated on sea front. Near Golf Course
and Bathing Pool. Adjacent to Tennis Courts and
Putting Greens.   H. & C. in Bedrooms.
"HOME COOKIN'" AND PLENTY OF IT

Under New Management   New Resident Proprietors:
Telephone: North Berwick 377   Mr. and Mrs. George McLachlan

CRAGSIDE MARINE PARADE

◦ Beautifully Situated on the Sea Front.
◦ Ideal Bathing Beach.
◦ Two Minutes from Golf Course, Tennis Courts,
   Putting Greens.
◦ Bedrooms—Hot and Cold running water.
◦ Separate Tables.
◦ Electric Light.
◦ Highly Recommended.
◦ Tariff on application.

Comfort assured under the personal Supervision of the Resident
Proprietors
OPEN ALL THE YEAR ROUND

MR. & MRS. E. SANETRA   Telephone : North Berwick 179

ARDVULIN
PRIVATE HOTEL
CLIFFORD ROAD · NORTH BERWICK

Situated near Station and overlooking Sea   Hot and Cold Water in all Bedrooms
Central Heating   Every Comfort Assured   Reduced Terms Spring and Autumn
Phone 384   Please quote this guide when writing   Prop. G. E. DILLON

Ardgay
MELBOURNE ROAD   NORTH B

'Ardgay' is situated in the East
Bay a short distance from the
Swimming Pool
It overlooks the Yachting Pond
and commands a lovely sea view
Convenient to the Golf Courses
and other out-of-door recreations

Reduced Terms for Children   Mr. and Mrs. T. N. Thomson
Telephone 534

Like other resorts throughout the country, North Berwick Town Council, through its Publicity Association, periodically produced a promotional handbook a 'Guide to North Berwick'. The guide was made available through Tourist offices, hotels and other similar establishments. The contents included a brief history of the Royal Burgh, the town's facilities and their cost (Visitors' Tickets for Bowling in the 1920s cost – daily, 1s 6d; weekly, 5s; monthly, 12s 6d.), a street map of the town, how to get there and the various public transport services available (in the 1920s a First Class return from King's Cross cost £7 19s 8d with Third Class costing £4 15s 10d), and numerous photographs of the town. Also included were brief details of local places of interest with their distance from North Berwick. Trade adverts of the shops, cafes and businesses also featured, along with page after page of boarding house and hotel listings like the ones left and above taken from the 1955 Guide.

Photographs in the early versions included photographs by Alexander C. Hutchison and James C.H. Balmain. One edition issued just after the Great War featured a number of Hutchison's photos, taken before the conflict, 'framed' with art nouveau decoration (see border). A later edition from the twenties not only featured many photographs of Balmain's work but was also produced by his studio in Station Road.

The guides were also a useful reference for locals and remained one of the Town Council's main tools for promoting the town until the 1970s.

85

Reginald Phillimore Phillimore

Reginald Phillimore Phillimore was born in 1855 into the middle-class family of William Phillimore, a medical practitioner at Nottingham Pauper Asylum. Phillimore was educated at the local public school and later at Oxford University eventually matriculating with a third class Honours in History.

From an early age he practised his passion for art – spending many holidays with his grandparents in Bridgnorth where he developed his skills. He shared his brother's flair for architectural drawing and combined with his knowledge of history concentrated his artistic activities to drawings, etchings and paintings of buildings of note and historical importance.

Following the death of his aunt, Emily Stiff in 1901, Phillimore inherited the Victorian end-terraced villa, 'Rockstowes', in Melbourne Road, North Berwick. It was there that he moved soon after and from where he built his publishing business producing postcards, etchings and books. His postcard sketches were hand-coloured by Mary Pearson, a local girl who later became his house-keeper until his death. Many of his postcards were printed on the continent in Germany in particular, and the range of postcards extended to over 700 in number. Many are of local East Lothian views and are very familiar because of his unique style, but most are of landmark buildings and views covering most of Great Britain. The business included the supply and delivery to a large number of outlets throughout the country and it is thought that at the publishing company's peak, there would have been as many as a million of the postcards in circulation at any one time.

His books included 'The Bass Rock – Its History and Romance' and 'Wizard of Tantallon', each of which came with over 60 decorative sketches.

Reginald Phillimore died at his beloved Rockstowes on the 24 December 1941 and was interred at the family vault in Bridgnorth, Shropshire.

Clockwise from above - Phillimore's sketches of Eider Ducks, Puffins, Razorbills, Cormorants and Gannets (Solan Geese).

Opposite page -
Top Left : North Berwick harbour with cargo boat and four fishing yawls.

Top Right : Storm off Bass Rock with fishing yawl LH 376 in the left foreground.

Bottom Left : Wreck at Tantallon.

Bottom Right : Quality Street.

THE HARBOUR
NORTH BERWICK.

R.P.Phillimore.

P.Phillimore

THE BASS ROCK
NORTH BERWICK

R.P.Phillimore.

TANTALLON

QUALITY STREET
NORTH BERWICK
156

DALRYMPLE

The Lodge

R.P.Phillimore

87

NORTH BERWICK FROM THE ISLAND OF CRAIGLEITH

View of North Berwick – A very spirited, and exceedingly artistic lithograph-drawing of North Berwick has just been published by Mr Hope, Edinburgh. The sketch is so minute in its details, that almost every building and neighbouring farmhouse can be distinctly made out. In the foreground, a picnic party are seated on the island of Craig Leith, from which point the view is taken. This familiar incident in the everyday experience of the visitors to North Berwick imparts much spirit to the sketch, and will contribute to render it a most agreeable souvenir of this much-resorted-to watering place.
Haddingtonshire Courier 9 August 1861

Picnics

Eating meals out of doors has been enjoyed for centuries but picnics, as we know them today, probably date from the early 1700s. Often grand affairs then where gentry were served their picnic on silver tableware by servants. In the 1930s and 40s they became informal and popular, particularly with the availability and accessibility to various forms of transport and with the growing interest in outdoor activities.

Above : Having completed their picnic on Elcho Green our well-heeled picnickers - the gents in their tweed suits with knickerbockers and the ladies in their cashmere twin-sets and tweed and Daks skirts - pose for the photographer before packing-up the tea-box of crockery and glasses into their open-top sports car. 1920s

Left : On the Isle of May on a beautiful summer's day, a group of young ladies have made themselves comfortable on their coats to enjoy their picnic which is laid out on a crisp, white tablecloth. Their trip to the May was with George Kelly, one of the North Berwick fishermen who supplemented his income taking groups out to the islands in the Forth. c1930

Sunday School Picnics

This splendid photograph shows Dirleton Church Sunday School picnic at Seacliff. The group comprises parents, children, a band, the Dirleton Public School Headmaster (lying front with his cap on his knee) and the Rev. John Kerr, Dirleton Parish minister (extreme right). 1900

Sunday School picnics in the late Victorian and early years of the twentieth century meant travelling to the picnic location by horse-drawn haycarts supplied for the day by local farmers. The horses were beautifully decorated with a prize of £1 for the best. Songs were sung to help pass the time and help forget the rigours of the journey. When the entourage reached a hill it meant – to ease the burden on the horse – all parents and adults having to jump off and walk. Congalton, Smeaton, Gilmerton, Biel and Seacliff were favourite spots that were easily accessible. Lunch was a bag containing a pie and buns. Races and football filled the afternoon with prizes of a few pennies. At Congalton, Mr Millar would lay on a few donkeys for riding. Tea was buns, scones and fruitcake washed down with home-made lemonade. Before leaving, a bag of conversation lozenges were scattered for the children to scramble for.

Later, buses were used to carry children to Humbie, Saltoun and other far-flung outposts of the County, and in the 50s and 60s little picnic bags of goodies were issued to each child, compliments of Mrs Culverwell, manager of Brodie's, the High Street bakers.

Top Left : Children from St Andrew's Parish Church prepare to leave for their summer picnic - possibly at Congalton. The carts are decorated with garlands and the horses have their manes and tails tied with ribbons. 1913
Top Right : Blackadder Church Sunday School picnic to Saltoun. 1967
Above : Abbey Church Sunday School picnic at Pressmennan. A table-cloth has been spread and the picnic eaten from china plates with knives and forks. However the lemonade can still be drunk straight from the bottle! 1911

Sand Modelling Competitions

From the very early 1900s, sand modelling competitions became one of the regular attractions of the visitors' 'season.' Held under the auspices of the North Berwick Town Council summer programme, the competitions were held on the West Beach three or four times through the season with the competitions normally attracting between one and two hundred entrants.

On the morning of the competition, under the supervision of the Burgh Surveyor, the beach was cleared of cartloads of seaweed, raked and marked out with as many a two hundred pitches, from the Elcho Slip westwards for 100 yards or so.

The contests were open to children, both local and visiting up to the age of fourteen years, and were split into different classes for the competition. Rules prohibited the use of anything other than products of the seashore although it was not unusual for some infringement of this rule. The event, especially if the weather was favourable, could attract a large gathering of many hundred spectators.

Above : For one local boy the first competition of the 1935 season was an opportunity to show his artistic talent. The competition, sponsored by the 'Daily Mail', was mainly to attract the children of the Edinburgh visitors. Our local boy came up with the idea of modelling a bird sitting on its nest with the following words written alongside -

'The bird has its nest
But we have the Daily Mail'

Including the sponsor's name was a brilliant idea. It won him first prize - 10 shillings.

SAND MODELLING COMPETITION

A COMPETITION

(PROMOTED BY THE TOWN COUNCIL)

will take place on the

WEST BEACH

ON

MONDAY, 25th JULY

Areas will be allocated to each Competitor, and will be available at 11 a.m. on day of Competition

THE MODELS WILL BE JUDGED AT 12.30 A.M.
EACH MODEL MUST BE FORMED SOLELY FROM MATERIALS AVAILABLE ON THE SHORE

PRIZES WILL BE GIVEN IN THE FOLLOWING CLASSES

1. Up to 7 years   3. 10 to 12 years
2. 7 to 10 years   4. 12 to 14 years

E. MENZIES, Clerk

Above : Crouching by her creation, this sand-sculptor looks delighted with her creation, although her friend, with head in hand, may not be so confident in its artistic merits. c1950

Above right : Standing to attention, this little boy is so proud of his work. And who can blame him? His pyramid crowned with feathers must surely deserve a prize! c1955

Above : For some, the wait for the competition judge could be a time to relax after a hard afternoon's work constructing a little palace with its own formal gardens. While for others (left) the wait for the approaching judges was a somewhat more anxious time - particularly if there was nothing to show!

Anyone for Tennis?

It was in August 1886, just nine years after the first Wimbledon Championships, when it was first proposed by Provost Brodie, that a piece of the Town's land behind the East Links should be levelled for the purpose of making a lawn tennis green. Unfortunately it was not until 1914 that public tennis courts were made available when four courts were constructed on the site as previously proposed.

The town courts were opened at 3.30pm on the 11th June 1914, on a beautifully fine afternoon with a competition involving eight players from Edinburgh, organised by Mr Smellie, secretary of the East of Scotland Lawn Tennis Association, with the first match including local girl, Miss Swan, St Baldred's Tower, playing off the first ball.

The price of a season ticket was set at 10/6 with monthly, weekly and daily tickets also available and with the courts open 6.00am until dusk. Mr David Matheson was appointed to act as superintendant at the courts and paid 30/- per week but employed only for the season which closed at the end of October.

Following their great success two further courts were added in 1919 and the following year the North Berwick Lawn Tennis Club was formed with an annual membership fee fixed at 15/6.

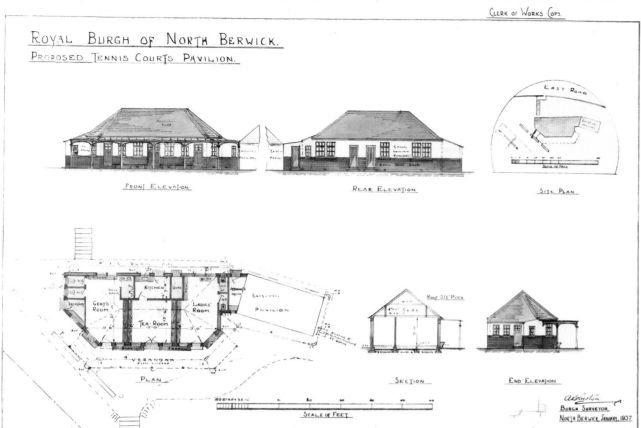

CLERK OF WORKS COPY.

ROYAL BURGH OF NORTH BERWICK.

PROPOSED TENNIS COURTS PAVILION.

FRONT ELEVATION

REAR ELEVATION

EAST ROAD

SITE PLAN

GENT'S ROOM

KITCHEN

SCORE

SECRETARY

TEA-ROOM

LADIES' ROOM

EXISTING PAVILION

VERANDAH

PLAN

ROOF 37½° PITCH

SECTION

END ELEVATION

SCALE OF FEET

BURGH SURVEYOR,
NORTH BERWICK, JANUARY, 1937.

Nº 7338

North Berwick
Public Tennis Courts

Half-Hourly Ticket 3d.

Left : Plans of the proposed extension to the Burgh Tennis Courts Pavilion by Andrew Robertson, the Town Council Burgh Engineer. The proposal with a glass-roofed verandah, kitchen, tea-room, secretary's office, and ladies' and gent's rooms each with adjoining toilets is very similar to the building that was actually built and which exists today. January 1937

TENNIS COURT & GROUNDS, ROYAL HOTEL, Nᵗ BERWICK.

Right : About 1906, a tennis court was constructed for guests of the Royal Hotel on the site of the old gas works cottage on what is now the parade of shops on Station Hill. Edwardian guests of the hotel - ladies in elegant full-length white dresses, wide-brimmed hats and white parasols and gentlemen in light summer suits and straw boaters - could sit on an elevated bank between the court and the hotel's other outdoor facility, a nine-hole putting green, and watch an energetic set or two.

EAST LOTHIAN OPEN TENNIS TOURNAMENT

The annual East Lothian Open Tennis Tournament began in 1927, when it was first run by the North Berwick Lawn Tennis Club in conjunction with the Royal Burgh of North Berwick Town Council. Mr. R. Kenyon Letts was the Men's Singles Champion with local lady, Miss Lulu Fowler, the inaugural Ladies Champion. Since then the Tournament has been run every year, except for an eight-year break, from 1940 until it was revived in 1948.

Up to 1975, when re-organisation of local government created East Lothian District Council (now East Lothian Council) the running of the tournament continued to be shared by North Berwick Lawn Tennis Club and the Town Council. However, this has evolved into today's format, which sees East Lothian Council, Tennis Scotland, North Berwick Tennis Club and Dunbar Tennis Club taking responsiblity for the overall running of the tournament.

In 1987, the tournament was nominated and chosen to receive the Scottish National Tennis Award for the "Tournament of the Year." It was then awarded the Tennis Scotland 'Tournament of the Year' in 2001 and 2011.

The tournament has grown in popularity, both in the number of events and the number of participants, and is normally held towards the end of July. In 1964, there were only ten events, growing to thirty-one events and 269 entries in 2001, and steadily expanding to 34 events (including a Wheelchair Tennis event) with 392 entrants in 2012 and this increase has meant the tournament is now one of the biggest in Scotland.

Above : Posters from 1928 and 1964 showing very different styles of promotion.
Below : Shortly after the Second World War, Tom Slawek (left), a member of the Waverly Lawn Tennis Club, began a seven year run in the gents singles. A Polish ex-airman, Slawek, was renowned for his perfect length ground-strokes. c1950

Three young happy 'mothers' setting out for a brisk walk along the beach on a cold winter's day. With their coats buttoned right up, it must be a concern whether their dollies will keep warm in the cold - particularly the one on the left which looks to have nothing but a thin sheet for warmth.

Previous Page : This posed photograph taken on the West Beach in 1902, during the celebrations to mark the Coronation of Edward VII in August of that year, shows a group of happy boys and girls all dressed in their best clothes for the celebrations. To mark their respect for the occasion they have busied themselves building an enormous sand castle which they have crowned with a Union Flag.

This lively group of Heriot Watt Students look to have the energy to entertain the whole West Beach on what is clearly a cold blustery day in 1933.

Above : We can only guess what this family have spotted. It has certainly caught everyone's eye. Perhaps Percy Pearson's fishing boat returning with fresh catch of mackerel, lobsters and crabs? c1934

Below : This photograph shows seven young friends posing for the photographer, George Day. Having raced home and changed into their best for the photograph they are now watching the incoming tide flowing around the piles of sand deposited by the Council's cart. During the winter, gales blow sand up against the sleeper-wall at the edge of the beach and in the spring it is removed down to the low tide level. c1952

Above : A photograph taken in the 1920s. The girls appear to have the West Beach to themselves on what looks like a cold day. At least their parasol adds an exotic touch.

Below : Four chums, with mischief in their eyes, pose for the beach cameraman in 1930. The Pavilion, in the background, can be seen while still under construction.

Fishing

Pleasure fishing and catching shellfish has always been a popular pastime with locals and visitors alike. Fishing off Galloway's Pier, the Platcock Rocks or harbour steps has always attracted children, particularly when Cllr. Norman Butterworth ran summer fishing competitions with prizes on behalf of the Town Council. Local children confidently knew where all the best spots were, especially when it came to catching 'partans' and lobsters down under the rocks at low tide using a stick with a hook attached to the end. Others collected sea urchins from the fishermen, scraping the spines off, cleaning them and giving them a coat of varnish - hoping to make a few coppers selling them to tourists.

Boat fishing was somewhat more exciting – out in the open sea with the prospect of bigger fish, perhaps cod down at the Bass or mackerel off the Craig. Today boats like 'Braveheart' not only take parties to fish, but also to scuba dive, bird-watch, sight seeing and to haul lobsters like the professionals do.

Fishing for 'dargies' and 'poddlies' from the harbour steps 1950s (top) and at low tide from Galloway's Pier (above) in 1931.

Local fisherman, George Kelly, willingly obliged requests from visitors to go out fishing hoping to catch a fish or two no doubt with an eye to the financial reward. On this occasion his delighted Edwardian guest has caught a plaice which she may have her cook prepare for lunch. c1910

28LB. COD CAUGHT

Mr Norman Butterworth, North Berwick, for many years president of the Edinburgh Deep Sea Angling Association, caught a cod with a six-foot split cane rod while fishing off Craigleith. On being weighed the fish turned the scales at 28lb. The previous heaviest cod caught with a rod was one of 18lb. 6oz. by Mr Balmain.

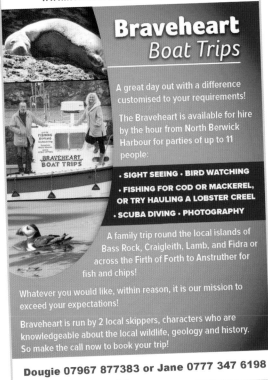

Above : Norman Butterworth with some prospective entrants to the Town Council fishing competition, which he so successfully organised. In the background can be seen a set of weighing scales which might come in handy if there is a large catch - with any luck possibly as large as Norman's 28lb cod he caught off Craigleith in the 1950s. c1960

North Berwick Sea Angling Club was formed in the early sixties with a couple of dozen members fishing from both boat, at St Abbs, Burnmouth, North Berwick and Gourock; and shore, with outings to Eyemouth, St Abbs, and Tyninghame. Fish caught included cod, haddock, whiting, ling, saithe, flounder, turbot, plaice and dab.

This little boy seems to know exactly what he wants to do when he grows up - be a professional fisherman like his grandfather. And what better way to start than by learning the craft of net-mending. His grandfather looks on proudly as the little boy, deep in concentration, tries out his sewing and knotting skills - 'filling a needle' for his grandfather who is mending a trawl net. c1950

Twentieth Century Accommodation

From the start of the twenties and through the thirties, particularly following the introduction of holiday pay, demand for holiday accommodation in the Royal Burgh reached its peak. Also about this time, death duties started to become a significant burden on the upper classes, resulting in many disposing of their high maintenance summer residences – although they still managed to come to North Berwick for the season albeit staying at the Marine or by 'taking a house'. This provided the opportunity for budding entrepreneurs from outwith the area to buy large Victorian villas to convert into boarding and guesthouses, with some others buying existing establishments like Chelsford House and Redcroft examples of each respectively.

'Chelmsford House', once home to the respected Dr Crombie, was opened as a guest-house by Miss MacKay in the 1920s. The large Victorian villa stands at the corner of Melbourne Road and School Road with commanding views over the East Bay from the Platcock Rocks to Jacob's Ladder, and with the golden sands of the east beach only a few yards from the front door. The accommodation provided for about twenty guests in the house with a further six in the converted stables - often referred to as the 'bungalow' - and was ideally located for a family holiday with all the town's attractions close at hand.

'Redcroft', a pension run by the Misses Snowden, was purchased by Maurice Vlandy, a Cretan from Hania, in 1919. Quickly, Vlandy established an excellent reputation and growing clientele. In 1924, he purchased additional land to the north to prevent further development in Ibris Place.

'Afterall I couldn't have people paying for a hotel and looking at washing,' he reflected after the purchase. To improve hotel facilities he built five tennis courts with their own pavilion and a putting green and by 1929 had extended the hotel westwards to provide 43 centrally heated rooms, all with hot and cold running water. Terms were a reasonable four to five guineas during peak season to a very modest £3 10s off-peak.

Top left : Redcroft, prior to the building of the new extension, showing two of the new tennis courts on what may have been the 'washing green' for the terrace of houses in Ibris Place with number 11 just visible (centre left). c1926

Above : Maurice Vlandy (top right), wife Mary (centre) and daughter Ella (front centre) in the garden of Redcroft with members of the hotel staff. c1920

Left : Miss Snowden outside 'Redcroft', a pension she ran with her sister. c1911

With the car unloaded and the family having refamiliarised themselves with the idyllic and wonderfully situated house, Vale Cottage, Forth Street (and garden), it was now time to take the children out to buy a well-earned ice-cream. 1950

Locals met the insatiable demand for accommodation with ingenuity and sacrifice. Every street in the town provided accommodation. Households were rearranged with "Are ye let?" a common greeting on the street in the Spring. For those that owned more than one house in the town it often meant flitting from the family home into the second smaller property – maybe the flat above the family shop, which had to be vacated by the winter tenant to allow the proprietor's entry. Household requirements were flitted round to the summer abode on the back of Bert Young's cart – the family home often having been pre-let to last year's visitors - with the children clambering on to the back of the cart for a 'hurl' - perhaps dreaming of being gypsies moving to a new site. For those with

Above : Taking a few moments to herself having cleaned her house from top to bottom, this landlady, in Melbourne Place, waits patiently in the sun for her next influx of visitors. 1930s

Top right : For this landlady (left) and her husband in Lochbridge Road it must have been somewhat disappointing to find their summer visitor turn up alone. Despite falling out with her husband their visitor (right) was intent on having her holiday. Happily all was not lost when her husband rolled up the next morning with his tail between his legs. 1935

Right : A group of visitors, with the men formally dressed in suits and ties with spotless shiney shoes and ladies, two in spotted suits and another three in cardigans and skirts, gathered together amiably on the doorstep of their Melbourne Road lodgings. 1930s

Page opposite : Annual lists of available accommodation were frequently placed in the house agents' guides. c1930

only the family home, it meant reorganising the living and sleeping arrangements, with mother and father often sleeping in the kitchen on a rolled out mattress. Children, if they were not sharing with the parents, may have camped out in the garden shed or a tent in the garden. It was even known for children of a family living in a tenement, to sleep out on the stair landing in the drawer of a tallboy. For some, their arrangements were unknown even to the neighbours, but speculation often led to fanciful tales like the couple who lived with their six children in a two-roomed dwelling in Market Place, but still managed to find a room for visitors. Rumour would have us believe the children were put to bed in the hall hanging from coat-hooks.

For those offering 'accommodation with attendance' which covered most of the more affordable lettings, this meant the landlady would be required to prepare all meals on a full-board basis with produce bought by the visitors. To ensure freshness, one visitor, a deliveryman with a firm of Edinburgh ice-merchants who delivered to the butchers and fishmongers along the Forth coast, was known to drop-off a block of ice along with the luggage the day before he and his family arrived for their two weeks. How long the block of ice lasted once it had been 'plonked' in the pantry Belfast sink no one can remember, but when there were no fridges they had to improvise.

'She would never have that at home!' was a common complaint among the landladies alleging that their visitors indulged in recipes during their holiday that the wives would never contemplate at home, resulting in the landlady being tied to the stove

---

LIST OF FURNISHED APARTMENTS TO LET
WITH ATTENDANCE

DIRLETON AVENUE

CAROLYN	Mrs. Law
INCHCROFT	Mrs. Galbraith
EGLANTINE VILLA	Mrs. Anderson
DUNIRA	Mrs. Elliot
KINGSTHORPE	Miss Smith

IBRIS PLACE

SUNNYHOLM	Mrs. Durie

MARMION ROAD

RAVENSHEUGH	Miss Hardie
SEAFORTH	Mrs. Mann
ARDGARTAN	Mrs. McKellar
ARGYLE LODGE	Mrs. Hutchison
CLAREMONT	Mrs. Pattison
No. 16	Mrs. Laing

ST. MARGARET'S ROAD

CROMLEIX	Miss Drummond

CLIFFORD ROAD

CRAIGILEA	Miss Patrick
ST. HILDA	Miss Flynn
MOUNTPELIER	Mrs. Givans
ACADIA	Mrs. Bee
No. 8	Mrs. McKemmie
10	Mrs. Dugan

Clifford Road—cont'd.

IVYDENE	Mrs. Morton
ROSEBANK	Mrs. Crawford
DURISDEER	Miss Cattanach

ST. BALDRED'S ROAD

TIGHNABRUICH	Miss Myles
HEDGELEY	Miss Lyle
NITHSDALE	Mrs. Burness
DOONHOLME	Mrs. Pow
CLOCHNAHILL	Mrs. Ross
YESTER	Mrs. Baillie
LANWYN	Mrs. Sutherland
BALWEARIE	Miss Durie

OLD ABBEY ROAD

FERNIEKNOWE	Mrs. Baillie
BONALY	Miss Borthwick
No. 3	Mrs. A. Russell
5	Mrs. J. Russell
7	Mrs. D. Russell
15	Mrs. Sawyers
25	Mrs. Pollock
29	Mrs. Richardson
VALETTA	Mrs. Goodchild
WINFORD	Mrs. Buckingham
8 ABBEY MEWS	Mrs. Forsyth

LIST OF FURNISHED APARTMENTS TO LET
WITH ATTENDANCE —cont'd.

ST. ANDREW STREET

SKEOCHWOOD	Mrs. Cummings
ROSEMOUNT	Mrs. Craig
HOLLIES	Miss Landells
JEAN COTTAGE	Mrs. Plimer
BOROONDARA	Miss Lees
BELTON COTTAGE (top flat)	Mrs. Virtue
No. 28	Miss Neilson
STRATHLEE	Miss Peacock

WESTGATE

No. 19	Mrs. Swan
47	Miss Morton
FIDRA COTTAGE	Mrs. Bannaford
SUMMERLEA	Mrs. Stewart

HIGH STREET

No. 10	Mrs. Oliver
32	Mrs Fender
39	Mrs. Blaikie
77	Miss Wood
78	Mrs. Scott
90	Mrs. Stitt
90	Mrs. Bell
90	Mrs. Grant
90	Mrs. Torrance
95	Miss Mason

High Street—cont'd.

98	Miss Stuart
98	Mrs. Allan
98	Mrs. Millar
104	Mrs. Kellas
107	Miss Morgan
117	Mrs. Fulton
124	Mrs. J. Herries

CHURCH ROAD

No. 1	Mrs. Sutherland

MARKET PLACE

No. 4	Mrs. Buist
4	Mrs. Black
4	Mrs. Gillies
11	Mrs. Bathgate

FORTH STREET

VALE COTTAGE	Mrs. Brodie
VALE END	Mrs. Lumsden
CAIRNFORTH	Mrs. J. Wilson
CAIRNFORTH	Mrs. Wilson
No. 36	Mrs. Soret
VIEWFORTH COTTAGE	Mrs. Small
LORNE SQUARE (off Forth St.)	
No. 1	Miss Cleghorn
3	Mrs. Balcombe
6	Miss Allan
7	Mrs. Ainslie

LIST OF FURNISHED APARTMENTS TO LET
WITH ATTENDANCE —cont'd.

MELBOURNE PLACE

No. 1	Mrs. Montgomery
25	Mrs. Laurence
25	Mrs. Burgon
25	Mrs. Whitelaw
25	Mrs. Harold
ARDMAY (Dunbar Rd.)	Miss McKellar

GLEN COTTAGES

Mrs. Bathgate
Mrs. Thomson
Mrs. Jardine
Mrs. Herries

LOCHBRIDGE ROAD

No. 2	Mrs. Smith
5	Mrs. Denholm
6	Mrs. Dickson
7	Mrs. Blackhall
9	Mrs. Nicholson
12	Mrs. Whitecross
14	Mrs. Wynn
15	Mrs. Forsyth
20	Mrs. Hutchison
22	Mrs. Duncan
24	Mrs. Combe
26	Mrs. Page
28	Mrs. Adams
52	Mrs. Samuel
54	Mrs. Kelly

LOCHBRIDGE

GLENLEA	Mrs. Staples
BEECHVIEW	Mrs. Aikman
BURNBRAE	Mrs. McLeod
BURNBRAE	Mrs. Lauder

GLENBURN ROAD

No. 3	Mrs. Denholm
8	Mrs. Brown
9	Mrs. Thomson
10	Mrs. Wallace
14	Mrs. Tait
15	Mrs. Laidlaw
16	Mrs. Harley
17	Mrs. D. Thomson
22	Mrs. Main
26	Mrs. Henderson
28	Miss Muirhead
32	Mrs. Davidson
33	Mrs. Anderson
34	Mrs. Lorimer
38	Mrs. Lillie
46	Mrs. Adams
48	Mrs. Allan
73	Mrs. P. Stitt
78	Mrs. Dunn

LIST OF FURNISHED APARTMENTS TO LET
WITH ATTENDANCE —cont'd.

QUALITY STREET

No. 10	Miss Millar
42	Mrs. Denholm
50	Mrs. Wallace

VICTORIA ROAD

No. 4	Mrs. Arundel
6	Mrs. Girdwood
8	Mrs. Dove
10	Mrs. John Miller
11	Mrs. Legget
19	Mrs. Richardson
THE POINT	Mrs. Costa

MELBOURNE ROAD

BEACH HOUSE	Mrs. Rae
SEASIDE COTTAGE	Mrs. Brash
LINDA VISTA	Miss Ballantine
INVERCRAIG	Mrs. Ramage
No. 16	Mrs. Ritchie
No. 16	Miss Currie
CRAIGARD	Mrs. Bell
FAIRHAVEN	Mrs. Stephen
DUNCRAGGAN	Miss Macfarlane
LYNBURN	Mrs. Carswell
SEAHOLM	Miss Brownlee
COILANTOGLE	Mrs. Orr
SKERRYVORE	Miss Johnstone

MARINE PARADE

ROSHVEN	Mrs. Duncan
ROCKVIEW	Miss Wilson
BLAIRELLEN	Mrs. Blair

EAST ROAD

No. 1	Mrs. Thomson
2	Miss McKellar
3	Mrs. Dooner

BALFOUR STREET

No. 9	Mrs. Whitelaw
9	Miss Sutherland
11	Mrs. Ainslie
15	Mrs. Cockburn
15	Mrs. Wilkinson
18	Mrs. McLaren
21	Mrs. Rollo
21	Mrs. Henderson
21	Mrs. More
24	Mrs. Smith
25	Mrs. Nelson
27	Mrs. Johnstone
27	Mrs. Robertson

for hours during the day. Many of the newly built council houses in Glenburn or Lochbridge were let with attendance. East Road at 12 o'clock was reputed to be like Blackpool 'prom' as visitors evacuated the beach and made their way to their lodgings for 'dinner.'

For all it was a worry if you were not let. Letting was the lifeblood of the town. The money, particularly during the Depression, helped make ends meet during the long winter months when father's income was short or non-existent with many children clothed and prepared for school on the proceeds from letting.

For the visitors there was the 'journey' – an exciting period of the year which for some started some weeks prior to departure, involving the planning, packing, arranging the uplift of luggage, and what to wear on the day. For those with access to motor transport the journey was relatively relaxed perhaps stopping en route for a picnic, anticipating the first sight of the Law, signalling the nearness of journey's end. For others, there was public transport which was no less exciting: peering out the window, also awaiting the first glimpse of the Law. For some it meant train connections and queuing to catch the North Berwick train, perhaps carrying a case filled with last minute rations, and for others catching a 2/9 return on a SMT bus.

Arriving was always thrilling whether it was entering the house 'taken for the fortnight or month' or for those lodging with attendance, renewing acquaintances with the landlady and her family – for many strong lifelong friendships started during the holiday, continuing in some cases for generations even when the visiting family ceased coming to the town. Once unpacked, for most, it was off out to reacquaint with familiar smells, sounds, and sights. For the children

it was an opportunity to spend some of their hard saved pennies - perhaps on a new bucket and pail from Howie's, the toy shop in the High Street or their first cornet from Capaldi's.

Following the hostilities of the Second War, visitors from the lower middle and working classes were no longer willing to accept cramped rooms. Many of the men had seen what had been on offer abroad and now expected more and better facilities when on holiday at home. The small private hotel was back in fashion. Many of the houses commandeered by the forces during the war were converted into family run hotels like Kings Knoll, smart family establishments with hot and cold in each guestroom. Along with the guest and boarding houses, the new family hotels absorbed all the lower-end demand with some operated by a small influx of Glaswegians, like the Stewarts who took over Chelmsford House. Rooms with attendance slowly petered out. However it was still the era of shared facilities and it was not uncommon for six or more guestrooms to share the same bathroom and toilet. And it still meant that the owner's family had to share smaller attic or basement rooms during the season.

Guests were given breakfast, dinner, high tea and supper and all for a couple of pounds. With no fridges, everything was bought daily and many of the shops delivered the goods to the door. Landladies' children would run up the street collecting morning rolls from Brodies, or to deliver an enamel pie dish to Eeles, left there to be filled with steak and kidney and later to be collected from Brodies who crusted the dishes, and on Saturdays trailing round the shops settling accounts. Visitors, as they had always done, returned year after year, with some following in the footsteps of their parents and grandparents - such was the draw, and still is the draw, of North Berwick.

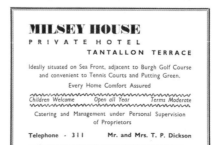

Right : Janet Dobbie, proprietress of Kings Knoll Hotel, overseeing a member of her kitchen staff, ensuring every detail is as a guest would expect. c1953

KINGS KNOLL HOTEL
NORTH BERWICK

In beautiful grounds overlooking sea: offers you all the relaxation of a perfect holiday. The bracing tang of sea and country to give you a full enjoyment of grand cooking. As much tennis, golf, swimming, riding or walking as you feel inclined for. A sun lounge for luxurious lazing, comfort that includes hot water in your room ; and all of it in the restful atmosphere of a country house by the sea

Personal Supervision
Early booking necessary for June, July and September
August already fully booked

Mrs. J. C. Dobbie   Telephone 442

King's Knoll, the house where King Edward VII stayed in 1902 was requisitioned during the Second War by the Forces. Thereafter for a period of over twenty years if was used as a hotel. The first page of the visitors book carries the entry - 'King's Knoll is the house of recline and pleasure, where the Masters make sure of you securing full measure, of all good things, that makes a holiday a treasure.'

Visitors were always happy to have their photo taken outside their holiday residence - sometimes just before they left for home (top right) or just as they were setting off (bottom right) for a morning at the swimming pond. Whatever the occasion by the 1940s the younger generation were dressing far more informally.

James Balmain, Photographer

Page Opposite : West Links, 2nd Tee. A photograph which for some epitomises playing golf at North Berwick during those halcyon summer days in the twenties and thirties.
Above clockwise from left : Miss Esmond and M. Deutach de la Meurtle; Earl of Egremont, J. E. Laidlay, Earl of Darnley; Sir George Rhodes; Sir Marshall and Lady Read, Sir Robert Aitken; Miss Alice and Sir John Lavery; the Countess of Oxford; Countess of Derby, Mrs Arthur Sassoon, Madam Leopold de Rothschild, and Her Grace, Countess of Wemyss. 1921 or 1922

James C.H. Balmain was born in Philadelphia of Scottish parents and came to Scotland in 1873 aged 19 where he soon found work as a vitro enameller with the celebrated Edinburgh photographer, James Tunny. Balmain was a photographic pioneer in the wet plate days of photography and soon opened studios in Shandwick Place and Salisbury Place.

In 1914 he opened his studio on Station Road, North Berwick directly opposite the station, in which he was eventually assisted, and later succeeded, by his son Kenneth. The purpose-built photographer's studio - later customised with large glazed panels in the roof - and adjoining house were previously occupied by the photographers Ernest Lippiatt, Peter Terras and John Ross.

Balmain took many photographs of local scenes but is probably best remembered for his photographs associated with golfing on the West Links golf course. Having struck up a friendship with Dan Stephen, the starter at the West Links, he was well placed to know when the aristocracy and other famous people of the day were due to tee off. Balmain took hundreds of photographs of the celebrities, which he sold either through the Press Association or directly to magazines like 'Tatler' and 'Vogue' and newspapers like the 'Daily Record', 'Sketch', 'Bulletin' and 'Sunday Pictorial'. His photographs of local views were licenced to postcard manufacturers and he also supplied the photographs for many of the Town Council Guides produced during the Twenties and Thirties.

Sir Victor + Lady
Warrender.

The firm of James Balmain captured North Berwick in photograph during its heyday, when the town was popular as a summer resort. The subjects included the West Links (opposite), a popular place to be seen, with the aristocracy and other society members filling morning tee times; the Burgh Course (above Left) particularly during competitions like the Colonel Weir Rosebowl, when crowds of spectators would regularly follow competitors around; summer storms (above right) whipped up magnificent waves which crashed on to the esplanade; sand-modelling competitions (centre right) when crowds of proud parents would gather around and admire the wonderful creations of their artistic children; street scenes - here with one of the first SMT buses to North Berwick (below right), parked in Quality Street, with a group of passengers having just disembarked and ready to take in a breath of sea air; swimming galas (below centre) with crowds thronging to the Platcock Rocks for the best views; and views - here from the Law (below left) prior to the developments on Mains Farm land, to the south of St Baldred's Road. c1930

111

Putting

Putting Course – Over 4000 players have during the past fortnight, patronised the new putting course, which like the tennis courts and swimming pond, also promoted by the Town Council, is proving a great attraction and financial success.

Haddingtonshire Courier 9 July 1920

The putting greens, close to the first tee on the West Links are exceedingly popular with summer visitors. Here, old and young may participate in a highly pleasurable pastime under the healthiest and happiest conditions. The charge is the moderate one of a penny per round, and putters and balls can be hired from the starter for an additional penny per round.

North Berwick Town Council Official Guide c1927

Putting competitions were a regular feature of the Edwardian summer entertainment at the Royal Hotel with exhibition matches between professionals a highlight. In August 1904, the month after his Open victory, Jack White played Arnaud Massey, the French Champion, and Ben Sayers in a challenge match over 36 holes – four rounds of the putting green that measured 100 yards by 30 yards. The match, which was for a purse of sovereigns, was won by Massey with a score of 92, with Sayers second with 93 and White with 99.

It was not until May 1919 that a town 'green' of nine holes – extended to 18 holes for 1921 season - was opened between Elcho House and the West Links, with the timber ticket pavilion constructed by William Auld & Son in 1931 for the sum of £49. A few years later a putting green was opened on the East Links adjacent to the tennis courts. Such was the competition between the course keepers, that the greens were comparable with the best championship golf courses.

In 1920 a putting competition for mixed-pairs was first promoted by the Town Council. Named after Councillor Loftus Calder, a butcher in the Westgate, the August tournament attracted a large entry of 120 competitors and was won by Miss N. Weir and Mr D. B. Swan. Eight years later it was agreed that the trophy would be competed for by singles rather than doubles, with the first prize a 'Benny' putter, won by Alexander Livingston. The same trophy is still competed for annually today, along with the Crawford Cup – a competition for under fourteens – in July over the East Putting Green with both, organised and run by the town's Community Council.

Other putting competitions were a regular feature of the Town Council summer events calendar, often sponsored by a national newspaper and attracting hundreds of entries.

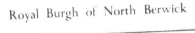

Below : Lawrie Lumsden, winner of the 1935 Calder Cup. His prize a 'Benny' putter 'every local golfer's desire.'
Right : 2012 ticket for one round £2.20.
Second right : 'Crawford Cup.'

Mr John Hooton (above) was appointed Putting Course Keeper for the East putting Course at a weekly wage of £2 10/- for the 1936 season.
North Berwick Town Council minutes
4th February 1936

Fancy Dress Parades

From the early 1920s the annual Fancy Dress Parade became one of the principal attractions of the summer season in North Berwick. Probably a successor to the cycle parades of previous years, participants dressed in every conceivable outfit imaginable from every corner of the globe, would employ all means of transport in their entry and they would gather on the East Links prior to the parade starting. A large number of collectors – usually for the Edinburgh Royal Infirmary - would accompany the procession receiving generous donations from the public who thronged to the streets to see the colourful and animated spectacle. Headed by an invited pipe or brass band the procession would wind its way around all the major streets of the town before returning to the East Links where the prizes were presented.

"The Young Bridal Couple", for which Miss Jean Brodie and Miss Nanny Duncan received first prize, was one of the best displays seen at the fancy dress pageant for some years. the 'bride and bridegroom' were seated in a pure white chaise drawn by a pony, and in front of them sat a massive white cake, while the vehicle was surrounded by many tiny trinkets, designed as wedding bells.

Haddingtonshire Courier 15 August 1930

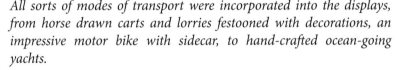

All sorts of modes of transport were incorporated into the displays, from horse drawn carts and lorries festooned with decorations, an impressive motor bike with sidecar, to hand-crafted ocean-going yachts.

After the Second World War the Fancy Dress Parades were revived in 1948 by the newly formed North Berwick and District Community Association. The pageant took the same form as before and was organised to raise funds for the Community Association. New prizes were awarded for Best Decorated Horse and Vehicle, Mounted Character, and Best Vehicle. The parade, which ended on the Coos' Green as previously, was followed by a demonstration of Scottish Country Dancing by the pupils of North Berwick High School under the instruction of Mr Spence with Miss Small on the pianoforte and Mr Bertram with the piano-accordian. Later in the evening there was open-air dancing on the harbour esplanade with music supplied by Dick Scambler's band.

The 1948 gala, showing the range of horses that was still available including the large farm horses. Until their demise in the post-war years with the entry of the 'wee' Fergie tractor, farm horses were a common feature at the galas with many beautifully turned out in ribbons and gleaming brasses. They formed an impressive sight as they pulled carts full of children in fancy dress around the town.

WE CONQUERED EVEREST

Entrants to the galas in the 1950s, 60s and early 70s were no less imaginative in their costume design - representing many walks of life from across the globe - many of which would have been devised, with the help of family and friends, over the previous days and weeks. The crowds were always delighted at the spectacle and the ingenuity shown in the costumes' preparation.

Mr. McCracken and the Warrender B.C. connection

James Hughen McCracken was born in the Dean Village, Edinburgh in 1884, the son of a gardener. On leaving school he started work as a butcher's boy, boarding in the Haymarket area of the city. In 1908 he was appointed Teacher of Swimming at Warrender Baths Club and it was during his involvement with Warrender, which endured for almost 50 years, that he discovered Ellen King and Jean McDowell, two of Britain's finest swimmers, both of whom represented Great Britain in the 1928 Olympics in Amsterdam. He also trained and coached Freddie Lemmon - who later became pond-master at North Berwick - giving him instruction in diving when young Freddie was expected to practise by diving from the rafters in Warrender Baths – into six feet of water.

In April 1920, McCracken was appointed pond-master of North Berwick Swimming Pond by the Town Council, for the forthcoming summer season with the agreement that he only work July and August, as he was full-time Swimming Master at Sciennes School in Edinburgh. His pay was to be £2 10s per week and he was allowed to keep all instruction fees and collections from any diving and swimming exhibitions he organised. From 1921 he was joined at the pond by his wife, Charlotte, who occupied a wee 'cubby-hole' behind the diving board selling hot Bovril.

McCracken was quite a large, dominant figure and although he could be quite abrupt he commanded a great deal of respect. At the pond he would invariably start the day taking the temperature of the water and writing it on his blackboard at the entrance to the pond. It was never warm, with temperatures as low as 48 degrees (F) not uncommon, even in summer. He was always dressed immaculately in white flannels and shirt, and almost always wore

Immaculately dressed, McCracken leading on competitors in a children's gala. 1930s

a black beret. A considerable amount of his time was given over to teaching lessons when it would be necessary - certainly when dealing with a novice - to pull on his body-waders and roll up his shirt sleeves and when teaching a pupil with something resembling confidence, employ his long bamboo pole. He was extremely strict and not frightened of threatening a nervous learner in the icy waters, often giving them a prod with his bamboo cane. It was not unknown for him to push his pupils in at the deep end, then shout to the poor floundering soul, "Grab the pole!" At which point his bamboo pole would enter the water just out of reach. Some of his pupils would howl when he started to bark at them if they did not do as he asked. This only made matters worse and he could often be heard growling, "I'll put you under the water." Then, almost at the same moment, he would wave across to the poor wee soul's mother and shout, "He's doing fine."

However it will be the successful swimming galas and the diving and swimming exhibitions for which he is most remembered. His contacts within the swimming world and in particular Warrender Baths Club enabled him to put on the most fabulous aquatic shows. He struck up an excellent working relationship with the stationmaster at North Berwick, so that on days when special visitor trains, full of excited factory workers, came to the town, the occupants could be directed down to the pond. McCracken, and his colleagues at Warrender, and to a lesser extent Portobello Swimming Club would be there to perform exhibitions in swimming, diving and water polo. The Council were delighted. He could do no wrong, even when he over-stepped the mark on the number of exhibitions he held, the Council turned a blind eye. Though free, each probably generated a pretty penny for him when the collections were counted.

The pond during McCracken's tenure, which lasted, with only the occasional break, for thirty-seven seasons, was one of the places to be seen. Despite his shortcomings, Jim McCracken played a significant part in ensuring North Berwick's continued success, and his name will forever be associated with North Berwick Swimming Pond.

Top Left : McCracken giving a reluctant diver a lesson. The swimmer attempts to stop McCracken pushing her in by wrapping her foot around his leg. 1937
Top right : A water polo match featuring Warrender Baths Club and a four-legged opponent. 1920s
Right : Mr McCracken giving a diving lesson with his trusty bamboo pole. 1930s
Below : Gala poster from 1930s

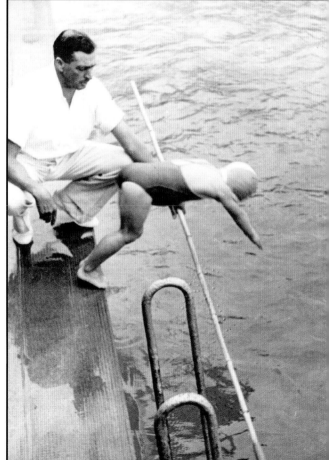

NORTH BERWICK SWIMMING CLUB

GALA
(UNDER E.D.A.S.A. RULES)

AT THE POND
Saturday, 9TH August
At 3 p.m. Gates open at 2.30 p.m.

Display by Naval Frogmen

Warrender B.C. v. Portobello S.C.
IN INTER-CLUB CONTESTS INCLUDING WATER POLO

Diving Display by Empire Games Representatives

Swimming Display by Warrender Ladies

Comedy Diving by Warrender B.C.

MUSIC ON THE ESPLANADE WILL BE PROVIDED BY
ROYAL NAVAL PIPE BAND

ADMISSION—ADULTS 2/- CHILDREN (under sixteen) 1/-
SEATS MAY BE BOOKED AT THE POND FROM 7th AUGUST

Swimming Pond - the Inter-War Years

For many people, North Berwick during the summer months in the twenties and thirties meant the open-air swimming pond. Open between 6am and 9pm weekdays - with restricted hours on a Sunday - the Pond was the heart of North Berwick. It was at the centre of summer activities for both residents and visitors. It was where it all happened! With its ideal location between the two bays, beside the harbour, sheltered by the Platcock Rocks with ample seating and standing places for spectators, it was little wonder that it was such a popular spot to spend an hour or two.

Many bathers took advantage of the early opening to have a swim before work which was particularly useful for commuters. For those visiting families who came for a month, it usually meant father commuted to work for one of the fortnights, so the opportunity for a swim prior to leaving for work was ideal.

Charges for the pond were moderate, ranging from 4d for a day ticket to 3 shillings for a season ticket. New dressing cubicles were introduced in 1930 as part of a scheme of refurbishment and improvement with those at the deep-end provided with electric heaters from 1935 at a charge of 4d, one penny more than the standard cubicle. The rather rudimentary slides and diving boards, which were acceptable before, were replaced with ones of modern design. Coloured fairy lights were erected above the pond which added to the spectacle of the evening galas and as the season drew to a close, and the nights drew in, there was no lovelier sight than when the pool was festooned with coloured lights shimmering on the pond's mirror-like surface. In 1936 a gramophone turntable was installed and it was the duty of one of the ticket-assistants to ensure it kept spinning with the record hits of the day – George Formby, Alan Jones, Deanna Durbin. Heady days, when the sun always seemed to shine on the pond at North Berwick.

Above : After a swim in the pool it was up to the sunbathing platform to dry off and size up 'the talent'. For locals it meant seeing who was visiting for the fortnight! c1925
Previous Page : The swimming pond in the early 1920s (left) with wooden changing huts. The two poles carried a rope pulley from which a novice swimmer was harnessed from the water, to learn to swim and (right) following the 1930 improvements with purpose-built individual changing cubicles.

The Motor Launches - 'St. Baldred', 'St. Nicholas' and 'Britannia'

From the end of World War One until 1920 no pleasure boat ran to or from North Berwick. It was only when Alex Hutchison applied to the Town Council in April 1921 "for leave to land passengers from a motor launch on the West Beach, when tide did not permit of these being landed at Galloway's Pier", that sailings returned. Initially working one boat it was only a few seasons before he started using two – the 'St Baldred' and 'St Nicholas'.

Hutchison's cruises took passengers either eastwards to the Bass Rock or westwards to Fidra. At Fidra, passengers were allowed to disembark for a short tour of the island. Conditional permission to land had been granted by Colonel Hamilton Grant, owner of Dirleton and Biel Estates, provided "only respectable people were landed" and "no dogs, firearms or spirits landed". Landing was at the small harbour, courtesy of the Commissioner of the Northern Lighthouse Board.

In 1929 with permission from the Town Council, Hutchison erected a small kiosk at the harbour where passengers could purchase their tickets. Hutchison, whose father was a keen photographer, was eager to maximise sales, and saw the opportunity to sell his passengers postcards made from photographs of scenes from the cruises, including gannets, the Bass Rock, Fidra Lighthouse, and views of the islands. The postcards printed by publisher J.B. White Ltd., Dundee, were bought in large quantities, such was the demand.

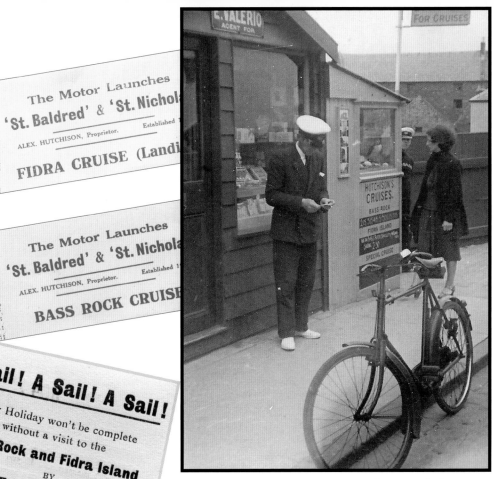

Page opposite : Preparing to tie-up the St. Nicholas. It looks like a quiet day with few customers about, and judging by the closed tented stage, certainly not sufficient to entice the pierrots to put on a show. c1925

Above : Hutchison's ticket office at the top of the lifeboat slip. Here Hutchison checks his tide charts while a member of his staff tries to entice a young lady to buy a ticket. The office, which was acquired from the Edington Trust, had a wonderful display of stuffed sea-birds by the local taxidermist, Willie Inglis, including a puffin which can be seen looking out of the window at an inquisitive passer-by. c1935

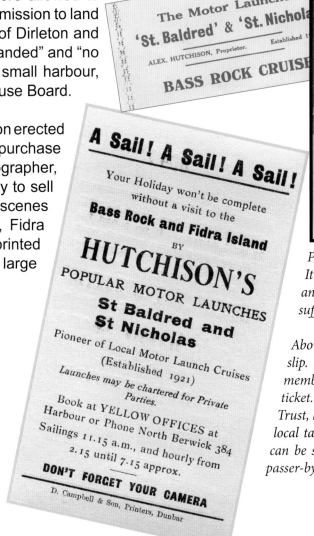

A Sail! A Sail! A Sail!

Your Holiday won't be complete without a visit to the

Bass Rock and Fidra Island

BY

HUTCHISON'S

POPULAR MOTOR LAUNCHES

St Baldred and St Nicholas

Pioneer of Local Motor Launch Cruises
(Established 1921)

Launches may be chartered for Private Parties.

Book at YELLOW OFFICES at Harbour or Phone North Berwick 384

Sailings 11.15 a.m., and hourly from 2.15 until 7.15 approx.

DON'T FORGET YOUR CAMERA

D. Campbell & Son, Printers, Dunbar

The Motor Launches
'St. Baldred' & 'St. Nichol
ALEX. HUTCHISON, Proprietor.   Established
FIDRA CRUISE (Landi

The Motor Launches
'St. Baldred' & 'St. Nichola
ALEX. HUTCHISON, Proprietor.   Established
BASS ROCK CRUISE

SPECIAL NOTE

THE
Local Motor Boats
'ST BALDRED' & 'ST NICHOLAS'
Are not Speed Boats

They are certified by the Board of Trade each Season, after test, as absolutely safe for Passenger Carrying for which they are specially built.

Page opposite : Bert Marr and Archie Thorburn, in their guernseys, outside their booking office, which is now entrance to the ELYC. c1938
Below : 'Britannia' returning with another boat load of satisfied customers. 1950s

Some years later, Hutchison's launches were joined by Archie Thorburn and Bert Marr's 'Britannia'. All three boats, which were of about 40 feet in length, were built by Weatherhead's at Port Seton and powered by Kelvin petrol-paraffin engines – the 'Britannia's' engine had been one of the exhibits at the 1938 Empire Exhibition held in Bellahouston Park, Glasgow. Extra bilge keels were fitted to help stabilisation for when the water became choppy out at the Bass. Each launch's complement was 40 including skipper and engineer.

The season started in the spring, about Easter, but was subject to the vagaries of the weather. When the boats could not run Thorburn, Marr and Hutchison had to return to their other trade of fishing, or in the case of Hutchison, sign writing and house decorating. All three boats ran trips out to the islands, Bass Rock, Fidra, Lamb and Craigleith, sailing in fine weather all day from 11.00am until 5.00pm. During the summer of 1939 there were visits to the waters off North Berwick from the Royal Navy ships which came in from operations and exercises in the North Sea. When they anchored in the west bay, they were a great tourist attraction with visitors queuing up to sail out to the navy boats. On one occasion, possibly in July 1939 there was quite a flotilla of navy crafts, which included cruisers and destroyers, and resulted in a continual stream of visitors to the harbour all looking to take a trip out in the pleasure boats to see the navy craft close-up. At the end of that summer when hostilities began, all business ceased.

The launches were requisitioned for active duty during WW2 as liberty boats and taken to Scapa Flow to tender allied sailors back and forth between the Orkney Islands.

At the end of hostilities the launches returned to North Berwick but in the post-war austerity it was difficult to run the boats profitably. In 1947 Alex Hutchison died, thereafter his son Ronald ran the business for a few seasons until David Tweedie, a retired submarine commander, bought the boats. Tweedie ran the launches until the summer of 1966, when he put the boats up for sale, with them eventually being sold in 1968.

126

PLEASURE CRUISES
BY
M·L· "BRITANNIA"

BOOK HERE

PLEASURE SAILINGS
(WEATHER PERMITTING)
By the New Super Motor Launch
'BRITANNIA'
(PASSED BY THE BOARD OF TRADE)

Leaving from the Harbour
at Intervals to BASS ROCK
FIDRA and OTHER ISLANDS

All particulars of the BASS ROCK
BIRD LIFE on the ISLAND

Passengers with Cameras
assistance to take Pictures

Special Terms for
OFFICE

PHONE 232

PLEASURE SAILINGS
(WEATHER PERMITTING)
by the New Super Motor Launch
'BRITANNIA'
(PASSED BY THE BOARD OF TRADE)

Leaving from the Harbour
at Intervals to BASS ROCK
FIDRA and OTHER ISLANDS

All particulars of BASS ROCK
and the BIRD LIFE on the ISLAND
explained. Passengers with
Cameras given every assistance
to take 'Pictures .....

ADVANCE BOOKING
For all CRUISES

BASS
ROCK
2-15
FARE 1/6
CHILDREN 9ᵈ

Above : Fred Marr at the bow of 'St. Baldred' with another boat-load of passengers all eager to visit the islands of the Forth to see the seals and abundant birdlife. The Port of Leith Pilot Boat, left, was a regular visitor to the harbour in the fifties and sixties. 1950s

Above right : 'Britannia' returning from Bass Rock with 'Craw' Pearson at the helm and 'Chieffy' Ling along side. 1950s

Top : A selection of the many cards Hutchison had produced from his father's photograph collection.

Above : Emboidered cap badges worn by Hutchison and his staff with that of M.L. St. Baldred depicting the monk, St. Baldred, with the Bass Rock in the background, and that of M.L. St. Nicholas depicting Father Christmas.

Right : Alexander Hutchison standing outside his booking office at the harbour. The kiosk gave Hutchison the opportunity to display photographs taken by his father, A.C. Hutchison, many of which he had printed as postcards. Such was the demand for the postcards that for the 1939 season he placed an order with the Dundee publisher of J.B. White Limited for 43 gross, 9 dozen and four cards, or 6,304 in total. The cost was £19 14 shillings or just over 1d each. c1929

Yachting Pond

A model yacht pond was first considered by the Town Council in March 1913. Unfortunately due to the outbreak of war it was not until 1922 when a pond was built. Completed at a cost of about £60, the pond lay to the north of Melbourne Road and measured about 60 feet square. Due to its popularity, and because the pond was in need of serious maintenance at the end of the decade, the Council proposed the construction of a new pond on a site adjoining the old one which was larger and deeper and more easily accommodated the larger vessels which were being sailed.

Sailing model yachts was a very popular pastime with both residents and visitors to the town from the twenties through to the early sixties – by both children, of both sexes, and grown men too. The Council funded two or three competitions annually throughout the season. Competition was fierce for both best model boat and race winner in each class of vessel. Some members of local families such as Auld, Henderson, Marr, Neill and Wightman built their own boats – either a scale model of a famous boat such as the 'Cutty Sark' or made to their own design.

Left : *The original yacht pond can be seen across the far side of the larger much improved new pond. In July 1933, the Town Council arranged a Model Yacht Competion with John Wightman, Willie Auld and Alf Patey to act as judges and with them determining the various classes and which prizes would be awarded. Larger yachts 10/-, 5/-, 2/6; smaller yachts 7/-, 4/-, 2/-; Mechanically propelled yachts 5/-, 3/-, 2/-; Decoration 5/-, 3/-, 2/-. All younger children received sweets. c1933*

Opposite page bottom left : Anxious 'wee' faces before a competition. Perhaps dress code was going to play its part in the judging of 'Best Model'. Locals were mostly smart casual with either wellies or bare feet and visitors more formal in blazers and sandals. c1948

Above : Jim Hutchison, second right, with his 'Milbro' manufactured metal-hulled Ailsa Yacht. In the competition Jim was winner of 'Best Model' and 1st in the race receiving total prize money of 10/-. The yacht's hull was polished with Simonize car wax to give a gleaming finish and speed through the water and the sails were brilliant white having been bleached by his mother. c1953

Above : MODEL YACHT EXHIBITION – Much attention is being directed this week to an exhibition of models of notable ships and yachts, and a collection of articles associated with them, which are on view within the spacious shop window of Mr William Auld, cabinetmaker, Westgate. In this display are four masted barques (including a fine model of the historic "Cutty Sark", brigantines, brigs, schooners, yachts of various rigs and types, and a perfect replica of a Cockenzie fishing boat. Never on this part of the coast has such a variety of models been brought together. They are the handiwork of some of the best-known modellists in Britain.

Haddingtonshire Courier 28 July 1933

Carl Henderson from Harmony Cottage in Forth Street was well known for making his own boats and was often seen pushing his splendid models to the pond down Victoria Road on a well-sprung pram chassis! As did Mr Halcrow, a dapper 'wee' chap from the top of Law Road, who would 'trauchle' down the hill with pram and yacht. Both allowed local children to sail their boats on their behalf. However, it was not necessary to have the skill of a cabinet-maker to produce a winner. Many local boys would fashion their own design made from whatever could be found - Jim Hutchison and Graham Thorburn entered and won a competition in the 1950s with their home-made catamaran – made with chestnut paling for the hulls, roofing slate for the keels and sails made out of an old school shirt.

Top Left : Down to the serious business of judging. Cllr. Butterworth inspected every entry in detail, its rigging, sails, and hull, before announcing the winners. Fortunately, everyone was a winner as the Council presented sweets to every entrant, as well as the main prizes. c1950

Below left : Most of the entrants look happy to have entered the pond competition on, judging by the parents' dress, what may have been a chilly day with one little boy actually radiating warm confidence. c1958

Page Opposite : The arrival of Mr Halcrow, the dapper 'wee' man in the white suit (top left) usually meant that the competitions were about to proceed. From the photographs it can be seen that there were some pretty large yachts entered, although they needn't be a concern if you were entering a battleship (top right).

Esmond Trophy

In August 1926, Mr John B Denholm, Captain of the Bass Rock Golf Club, wrote a letter to North Berwick Town Council, informing them that the club intended fixing an annual golf competition open to all artisan players in the County. As prizes Denholm had secured two gold, one silver and two bronze medals along with a magnificent silver trophy in the form of a reproduction of Edinburgh Castle. All were the generous gifts of Mr Edouard Esmond with a view to encourage golf among the artisan classes in the County.

The competition, was to be held over the Council's Burgh Links which, following Denholm's request, were given freely for the competition by its owners. The competition comprised an 18-hole qualifying round with the first 16 from that round entering a match play competition over three eliminating rounds and the final two playing for the splendid trophy and gold medal on Saturday 26th September. The inaugural 1926 competition was won by Hugh Watt, a member of Dirleton Castle G.C.

On the evening before the tournament commenced the Esmond family invited members of the Bass Rock G.C. up to their summer residence at Marlyknowe. There, tea and sandwiches were served and later a friendly putting competition took place over the green at the side of the house. Each member was given a packet of cigarettes and a golf ball prior to their leaving.

It was a couple of years after the Second War until the part of the Burgh course used in the war effort was brought back into play. During that period the tournament took place over the West Links. The same course was again used in 1961, and from 1968, when entrance requirements to the competition were altered to allow all members of the East Lothian Golf Clubs to compete, play was switched to the West Links on a permanent basis.

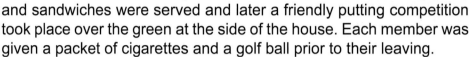

Top : Winner's gold medal depicting Edinburgh Castle.

Top Right : Edouard Esmond, an enthusiastic golfer, and his family were regular summer visitors to the town spending many months at their summer residence, Marlyknowe.

Far Left : The Esmond Trophy – a replica of Edinburgh Castle - is a magnificent piece of workmanship executed by the Regent Street firm of Goldsmiths and Silversmiths Company Ltd (amalgamated with Garrard & Co in 1952).

Left : The 1948 winner, A F Hutchison, was presented with this silver trophy, by the Edinburgh firm of Hamilton and Inches, in place of the usual gold medal.

Some of the Esmond Trophy winners, clockwise from top left : James Brash, 1929; Harry Stewart(right), 1993, with James Brash; Archie Denholm, 1951 and 1963; Ritchie Bathgate, 1971 and 1983; Peter Craig(left), 1956, with John Holm; Rab Arundel(right), 1960, with l-r : Dennis Millard, John McNair and Harvey Butterworth; John Fender, 1938 and 1946, with Mrs Esmond (left); Hugh Watt, 1926; Peter Miller, 1984; Vic Logan(right), 1967 and 1968, with Ritchie Bathgate.

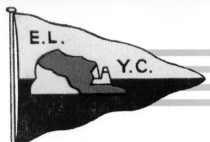

East Lothian Yacht Club

East Lothian Yacht Club was formed in 1928 and held its inaugural race, possibly the first dinghy race to be held on the east coast of Scotland, on the 13th June 1929. The club was formed by yachtsmen in North Berwick and the County for the purpose of encouraging yachting on the East Coast, and membership was open to children from the age of ten.

The Club's fleet of seven dinghies, all called after ladies' Christian names, were designed by the internationally renowned Glaswegian yacht-designer Alfred Mylne. Built by Messrs George Brown & Son, Leith, they were known locally as '12s' – after their length of twelve feet, but more commonly as 'Forth Class' or 'Brown Class' dinghies.

The racing course for the first race – an equilateral triangle of two miles – was laid out by committee members Calder and Whitecross with the results of the race as follows :- 1. 'Joan', (Sir Patrick Ford M.P.); 2. 'Fiona', Miss Betty Montgomery; 3. 'Amy', (Mr R A L Balfour and Dr Wedderburn); 4. 'Jean' ((Dr J C Dunlop); 5. 'Helen, (Mr L Calder and Mr Inglis); 6. 'Inez', (Miss Eileen Tweedie). Later as a result of a protest upheld by the Sailing Committee, Mr Calder's boat was placed third.

12s continued to be used by the club until the 1960s.

Above : Storing 12s for winter. c1950
Above Right : George Brown & Sons' brochure including "Forth" Centreboard Sailing Dinghy - known locally as 12s - costing £25. 1950s
Bottom Right : The start of a '12ft.' dinghy race. c1950

THE "FORTH" CENTREBOARD SAILING DINGHY.

Length overall—12 ft.

Beam—4 ft. 6 in.

Depth—1 ft. 9½ in.

Capable Sailing Dinghy which is also quite suitable for rowing or for a light outboard motor.

Yellow Pine Planking with Mahogany Topstrakes.

Centreboard ⅜-in. galv. plate.

Sail area—85 sq. ft.

All plank fastenings of copper or brass. Finished three coats best yacht varnish. Complete with one pair spruce oars, rowlocks, etc.

Price—£25 0 0

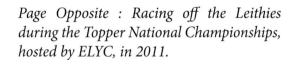

YACHT DINGHIES.

Suitable for rowing or towing, and also suitable for a light outboard motor.

Oak scantlings.

Silver spruce planking.

Mahogany topstrakes, transom, thwarts.

Canadian Rock Elm timbers.

Complete with pair of leathered spruce oars, rowlocks, etc.

Copper and brass fastenings. Finished three coats best yacht varnish.

10 ft., £12 10 0	11 ft., £13 10 0
12 ft., £14 10 0	14 ft., £17 0 0

Page Opposite : Racing off the Leithies during the Topper National Championships, hosted by ELYC, in 2011.

From the late fifties general purpose dinghies - GP14s and Graduates and later Mirror dinghies - made from plywood became available and proved very popular. This made sailing more available to all, particularly here in North Berwick with the new dinghies capable of being launched directly from the beach whatever the height of tide.

In recent years, sail training for both adults and youngsters has formed an important part of ELYC with the club aiming to introduce as many people as possible to the enjoyment of the sport of sailing, and to help them progress and develop. The club has its own fleet of 12 Toppers, 4 Fevas and 4 Laser 2000s available for use by members, be they novice or experienced sailor.

A registered Community Amateur Sports Club, the club today is entirely run by volunteers, and at a national level is held in the highest possible regard. Its location at North Berwick, with its excellent open sailing water with easy access, and its willing and able pool of vounteers, has in recent years allowed the club to host various classes in National Dinghy Championships. Already various championships are booked for the coming years. The occasion of a championship in the town, which has become almost an annual event, provides a significant cash injection through the accommodation and board requirements of competitors - who come from throughout the UK - both locally and in the neighbouring towns and villages.

Caravanning

Caravanning started to become popular after the end of the First War with the earliest caravans adapted or converted from gypsy and agricultural wagons and carts. Later military vehicles, old disused railway carriages and old omnibuses were pressed into service. Often the 'caravan' would be pitched on a farm with Scoughall and Bass Rock Farms popular sites in this area. There it would remain for many years – more often than not until it was no longer fit for use – to be used by the owner and his extended family throughout the year.

Opened in the 1920s, Scoughall Caravan Park extended from Scoughall Cottages all along the links to Pefferside, a distance of over ½ mile. The first caravan there was owned by the Heatly family and by the late 1930s the site comprised a conglomeration of over 100 old huts, tents, buses, wooden chalets, and gypsy caravans of all description, even a tramcar. One caravan, more than likely 'home-made', was completely round, on wheels that ran on rails. It could be turned, like a roundabout, to ensure the windows always faced the sun and was always a hit with the children who scrambled aboard for a ride when it was being turned.

The owners, mainly from Edinburgh, but as far afield as Glasgow, came down in the better

Above : An Edinburgh family, take a break at Horse Crook, en route for a family holiday at Scoughall. 1920
Right : Scoughall Caravan Park with its proliferation of buses, railway carriages, huts and tents. c1930

weather. Some came by car, some by bus – dropped at the road-end - and some by bicycle, with many, cycling from Glasgow for the weekend!

Groceries and newspapers could be had at Dalgleish's store situated at the end of Scoughall cottages. Water was the only service provided from a row of stand-pipes put in by Hugh Gibson's Heirs, the Leith plumbing firm owned by the Heatly family. During the Second World War the caravans were commandeered for the Polish troops and because they were in such poor condition after the war the site was cleared and not reopened.

A putting green at Scoughall was laid out by Jock Dale and maintained by Sandy Chalmers. Children played for free, more often with up-side-down walking sticks than with proper putters, with the men paying a few coppers to Sandy. In the distance some of the various assortment of styles, shapes and designs of 'holiday home' which were located at Scoughall can be seen. 1938

Above left : Having arrived safely at Scoughall, time for a tune on the accordian and a 'wee' song. c1930

Above top : Once settled-in, having erected additional accommodation in the form of a large circular canvas tent, and after the long slow trip down from Edinburgh, the caravanners could think about more leisurely pursuits like tennis. c1930

Above : With the washing and other chores done, time for a walk down to the beach to try out new wellies. c1930

Left : A number of visitors sited their caravans at the Bass Rock Farm at the top of the Heugh. Really a collection of gypsy caravans, a bus, tents and other erections, they were used mainly in the summer months but a few were occupied year round by individuals who had fallen on hard times. Visitors often had to carry-out essential maintenance - painting the steps to their gypsy caravan and ensuring the fence would hold back any inquisitive cow - before they could start to enjoy their holiday. But there was always the evening meal to look forward to on long glorious summer evenings. 1930s

Above : Previously known as 'The Bungalow', refreshment rooms belonging to clubmakers A. & J. Marshall, 'May View', on the Dunbar road, was a small site established in the thirties for tourers. With only room for a few 'vans it was more than large enough for passing tourers, as they were still relatively uncommon. 1950s

Left : The official 1967 guide to North Berwick described the caravan site at Rhodes Farm run by the Town Council as one with real amenity - maintained to a high standard with facilities including hot water and showers. The site, which was open to members of the Caravan Club only, sat on an elevated site above the East Bay, with commanding views over the town and Forth islands and across the Firth to Fife.

Your kind of holiday ...
WITH YOUR CARAVAN

IF your kind of holiday centres around a caravan, but demands all the amenities and comforts of a good site and all the attractions and facilities of a fascinating seaside resort, then North Berwick provides the simplest and most satisfying answer to your holiday problem.

First, you have no towing problems—from all over Britain, first-class roads lead to North Berwick.

Second, there are two sites at North Berwick—both on the main North Berwick-Dunbar road, close to the town. The 'Rhodes' Caravan site is open to members of the Caravan Club only and of course all the usual facilities can be found there.

The other site which is open to non-members of the club is adjacent to the recreation park. Charges:—3/6 per night, £1 per week.

Dr Robert Macnair purchased the old North Berwick 'Fever' Hospital in the 1930s with the intention of opening a convalescent home, catering to the patients' vegetable needs in the adjoining field. However, recognising a need to satisfy a growing demand for caravan sites, Dr Macnair developed the field into North Berwick's first caravan park, renaming the park 'Gilsland' after the town in Cumbria.

Caravaning, both static and touring, was still in its infancy with caravans rare and expensive to purchase. Caravanners had to improvise with other vehicles and this led to the arrival at 'Gilsland' of such quaint oddities as an Edinburgh Corporation bus and a railway carriage. Both were converted to provide comfortable holiday accommodation and were amongst the first 'static caravans' on the site.

Closed for the duration of the Second World War, the park reopened soon afterwards and became popular with regulars from Edinburgh and Fife, many of whom would come down for the weekend throughout much of the season. Water was available from a stand-pipe at the top of the field and everyone supplied their own 'privy' and attended to the same. The annual rent for the pitch was a very reasonable £12.

It was in the 1950s, with the availability of affordable motor-cars, that caravanning became progressively more popular. The implementation of legislation, including the Caravan Sites and Control of Development Act 1960, enabled local authorities to license sites and encourage improvement. Site facilities improved dramatically with toilet and bathing facilities mandatory.

Gilsland was eventually cleared of the old static homes – the buses, railway carriage and other huts – and a new toilet block installed. Later a new field was opened, paying shower blocks and laundry installed, and a site shop opened.

Below : 'Gilsland' in the sixties with the original field filled with a variety of tourers of all shapes, sizes and vintages. The new shower-block and toilets can be seen centre.

Swimming Galas - the Inter-War Years

Aquatic Gala c1920 - note that the pierrots are not performing during the gala as they were precluded under the terms of their contract with the Council.

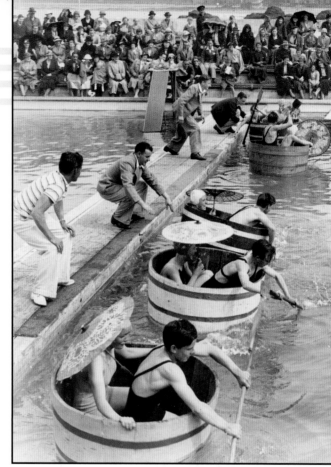

Starting the barrel race from the boom with the passengers sheltering from the rain under their chinese parasols. We can only guess whether they reached the finish mark still afloat. 1922

A major feature of the summer season at North Berwick was the spectacular swimming galas held under the auspices of North Berwick Swimming Club or Town Council and organised by the pond-master. Following the success of the demonstration of swimming and diving at the opening of the pond in 1900, displays of aquatic skill, speed and fitness along-side acts of tomfoolery became a regular summer feature at the pond. The galas, with three or four held each season, would also include trick and artistic displays of swimming, novelty races with wooden horses, barrels and other props, with the home club competing against one of the Edinburgh clubs. Usually an exhibition match of water polo between the two clubs would end proceedings with music provided during the event by North Berwick Pipe Band.

The opening gala event of the season would often be the end of term presentation by local school children with an invitation inter-scholastic team race between Dunbar, Preston Lodge and the home team. This could be followed by a life saving display by senior girls. Later during the school holidays, the pond-master would organise swimming competitions with races between local and visiting children.

During the galas, as well as the usual races and diving competitions, displays were given by visiting professionals: with divers such as Peter Desjardins, Harold 'Dutch' Smith, Jimmy Rae and Hank Akers;

1937

Above : Winners of the girls under seven race receiving their prizes from Baroness de Waldner. 1937

Below : A packed house of mainly proud parents cheer on competitors entering for the children's gala which included races for tiny tots and learners, and also Rhythmic Exercises by pupils from the High School. c1928

Peter Desjardins 1928 Olymic Diving Champion

log rollers like W. C. Bradborn; and swimmers like Ellen King, the Scottish Olympian and winner of two silver medals at the Amsterdam Games in 1928.

Desjardins, an American who represented his country at the Olympics, winning silver and gold in the 3m springboard diving competition at the '24 and '28 games respectively, was a regular visitor to our shores, and visited North Berwick several times in the thirties. His fee, negotiated by his agent E. J. Larkins, was about forty guineas inclusive of hotel and travelling expenses. This, like many of the other touring performers, covered extra displays during normal pool hours when children had the opportunity to compete against the stars - like "doing a Johnny Weissmuller" off the top board with Pete Desjardins, where each ran up to and off the end of the board and parachutted down to the pool with open parasol in hand. A gala usually ended with food tins thrown into the pool for children to dive for. It was useful during the war to be able to take home a tin of fruit or meat to mother without using up ration vouchers.

In the 1920s evening galas were introduced, which included performances of 'elegant swimming' (synchronised) by local schoolgirls who had been tutored by Mr. McCracken. The girls performed their routine in smart white swimsuits, donated for the event by Sim's, the High Street draper, and which reflected the twinkly bright colours from the fairy lights dangling above. The finale, a grand firework display by Mr George MacKenzie from Edinburgh, and funded by the Council to the tune of £15 ended a entertaining evening.

During those two decades between the Wars, the swimming pond was a very special place. Whatever the weather, a gala at North Berwick, unlike anywhere else, would still attract a large audience, even on a cold wet night with the wind howling.

Top Left : Jim McCracken, pondmaster, introducing the competitors to the packed 'house' during a children's gala in the summer of 1937.

Top Right : A spectacular firework display at the end of the final gala of the season brought another summer season at the pond to an end. Whatever the weather, galas held at the swimming pond in North Berwick always attracted huge audiences.

Main Page Opposite : On a cold September evening in 1934 the final electrically illuminated gala of the season took place during which the Lyall sisters gave an exhibition of Graceful Swimming to a packed audience of hundreds - Roberta, whose first exhibition this was, Jean, 1933 Graceful Swimming Champion of Scotland, and Mary, 1933 Graceful Swimming Champion of the East of Scotland.

Bottom Right Page Opposite : Senior girls from North Berwick High School ready to take part in a Life Saving Display. 1931

Fishermen's Friends

The harbour has always been a popular destination - always having something of interest to catch the visitor's attention. Ben Millar (above) is observed by a group of school girls on the art of making a creel, 1930s. George Kelly and Alf Marr (top right) have been persuaded to take some local girls from the telephone exchange out to the islands in their fishing yawl, 1930s and (right) Percy Pearson looks to be enjoying the company of some young Edinburgh University students who are taking a break while out collecting monies for 'Rag Week'. c1947

146

Sandcastles

It is every young child's delight on a visit to the beach, when given a bucket and spade, to start work on the largest and prettiest construction ever seen on that particular stretch of sand. Incorporating seaweed, shells, pebbles and other valuable building materials freely available from the beach and rock-pools, hours of pleasure can be spent designing, constructing and decorating a castle or palace fit to live in.

Above : Down to the bare-essentials, this 1980s trio are preparing for a day's building - starting with assessing equipment and a suitable place to start.

Below : Disappointing, after a day's graft, to see your castle flattened by an incoming tide. Not to worry, tomorrow is another day and a newly levelled-building site will allow an even bigger castle. 1950s

Happy in her work, this 1920s builder has taken time off to search the rock-pools for suitable decoration.

This 1920s builder, in her pretty floral dress, cardigan and new sandals, is clearly still waiting approval of her endeavours from her mother and granny, both suitably rugged-up against the cool sea-breeze. Unfortunately the castle seems to have suffered a little subsidence while waiting to be 'signed-off'.

Redcroft Challenge Cup also known as The Esmond Cup

Above : Play during an early 'Redcroft Challenge Cup' tournament in the late 1920s - the ladies playing in skirts mid-calf in length and the gents in full length 'whites'. On the right of the photograph, taken by the firm of James Balmain, is the new pavilion recently opened by Sir Hew Dalrymple while guests and visitors can be seen being served refreshments by an aproned member of Redcroft staff. The land beyond the hedge, which bounds Ware Road, was later developed into Lord President Road in the 1980s. On the skyline just visible amongst the trees is Cheylsmore Lodge.

Right : The silver 'Redcroft Challenge Cup', Art Deco in style, was designed and made by the reputable George Street firm of Hamilton and Inches. It was played for annually until the summer of 1939 - only three weeks before the outbreak of World War Two.

Tennis tournaments were a regular feature of the Redcroft Hotel summer diary with the 'Redcroft Challenge Cup' being the highlight. The trophy, a present to the hotel proprietor Maurice Vlandy by his friend Edouard Esmond, was also known as the Esmond Cup and was first played for in 1927. The competition, held on a Thursday afternoon in August, was American Mixed Doubles Handicap, and was very popular with visitors and locals drawing a large entry.

Above : Mrs Esmond with the winners and runners-up of the 'Redcroft Challenge Cup' tournament. 1930s
Top Right : Some of the young ladies awaiting their partners before the start of a 'Redcroft Challenge Cup' tourney with Maurice Vlandy (2nd right) looking on. 1930s

Above and Right : Maurice Vlandy, proprietor of Redcroft, organised an annual charity tennis competition in aid of Donaldson's School for the Deaf and here we see some of the young competitors. 1930s

The Pavilion

Consideration was first given to a public hall at the harbour by the Town Council in 1928, on a site to the north of the Anchor Green formerly the site of the old town stables and yard. Following a tendering process, an offer and plans drawn up by the Glasgow building firm of D. McKellar were provisionally accepted in autumn 1929. After a number of consultations with the builder which resulted in some modifications to the plans, approval was finally given at the turn of the year for work to commence. On the 30th June 1930 the new Pavilion, as it was to be called, was formally declared open. Although unfinished, the Council were of the opinion that the hall should be opened. The Pavilion, which was built at a cost of £3042:14:10, was of an ornate and elaborate design and large enough to accommodate 450 people with seating by way of tie-up chairs. The hall, with its lofty ceiling, was well ventilated with a stage and changing rooms at the south end, and a tearoom for the provision of refreshments and kiosk for the sale of cigarettes and sweets.

Following the opening ceremony which was conducted by Provost Eeles, the invited audience were entertained to a performance by Fred Luker and his Zenith Entertainers. Luker, a former manager and producer of entertainments at Dunbar Pavilion, and his troupe were providing the entertainment on the Esplanade that season and following the opening ceremony the troupe gave a performance which met with much enthusiasm, calls for encores being frequent.

Once complete, apart from being used for the summer season's daily entertainments, the hall was expected to serve the community throughout the remainder of the year for various events and functions – amateur dramatics, school plays, badminton, and many social events and engagements. Dancing was always popular, with women sitting down one side and the men the other. At the start of a dance the men would walk over and ask a lady to dance. For a number this was how relationships started with some leading to many happy years of marriage.

Left : Fred Luker, with his troupe, Zenith Entertainers, before a performance at the Pavilion. 1930

Below : A packed house enjoys one of the many variety shows held during the summer season. The shows included dancers, ventriloquists, comedians and singers, with some performing at both Dunbar and North Berwick on the same night! It meant dismantling stage equipment, loading up transport, rushing over to the next location and preparing everything to go on stage again. c1958

The summer season entertainments at the Pavilion ran from mid-June through to September and over the season a variety of acts was booked through the Town Council's entertainment officer. Many were familiar from television and radio with regulars from the 'White Heather Club' prominent as the headline act during the late fifties and sixties. During the day children's shows provided relief for the visiting parents when the weather was inclement with Aunty Dot a particular favourite. Her show, usually twice weekly, was a great hit and was a regular fixture throughout the summer for a number seasons.

ROYAL BURGH OF NORTH BERWICK
PRESENTS
SUMMER SEASON ENTERTAINM
Commencing Tuesday 19th June, 1962

TUESDAYS, WEDNESDAYS, THURSDAYS
at 8 p.m.
THE NORTH BERWICK
FOLLIES
STARRING SCOTLAND'S OWN
DAVE WILLIS ★
WITH SUPPORTING
Artistes
PRODUCED BY
JEAN KERR

CHILDREN'S
PLEASURES
Tuesdays & Fridays
at 6 p.m.
CHILDREN'S CORNER
FUN, GAMES AND MAGIC
WITH
AUNTY DOT & GUEST ARTISTE

DANCIN
To the Mu
THE M
DANCE
with M
Fridays : 9 p.
Saturdays : 8.30

H OF NORTH BERWICK
PAVILION
WEDNESDAY, 27TH MAY - 7-30 P.M.
GRAND PRE-VIEW SHOW OF 1959
SUMMER ENTERTAINMENTS
ONE PRESENTATION — 3 HOURS
FOLLIES
OF 1959
Jimmy Stevens — Compere
Maysie Forrest
Howard Whitehead
Lottie Russell
Bill Toall
Sheila Reid
Jackie Lawrence
The Brandon Four
Comedy - Song - Dance
JEAN CARNIE'S LADY
PIPERS AND DANCERS
A Highland Treat

SCOTTISH NATIONAL
OPERA COMPANY
Musical Director:
BEATRICE MIRANDA
Popular Music from
Musical Comedy & Opera
40 ARTISTES
Music by
JIMMY McINTOSH'S
BROADCASTING BAND
ADMISSION - 3/-

A Show for All the Family
A BREATH OF SCOTLAND
Your comedy host
RONNIE COBURN
THE GLENGARRY DANCERS
GILLIAN CAVIN and JIMMIE NICHOLSON
Our young Music Maestro
MIKE CLARK
CHRIS KENNY and
GILLIAN MURRAY
Come and join us in the Ceilidh
BILLY MARSHALL
Scotland's Singing Minstrel
Tickets £1.50 Senior Citizens, Children and Unemployed £1.00
Victoria Ballroom, Dunbar
Tuesdays, July 6, 13, 20, 27, August 3 and 10
Harbour Pavilion, North Berwick
Thursdays, July 8, 15, 22, 29, August 5 and 12

THE
PAVILION
NORTH BERWICK
Commencing MONDAY, 17th JUNE
ERY MONDAY, TUESDAY and WEDNESDAY at 8 p.m.
THE NORTH BERWICK TOWN COUNCIL PRESENT
Radio, Television and Recording Star
BILL McCUE
who says
IT'S A FINE THING TO SING
With the Lovely Singing Star from Television's "White Heather Club"
MOIRA ANDERSON
AND FEATURING THE
JIMMY SHAND Jnr. TRIO
With TOMMY LEES and TOMMY ARNOT
At the Piano JILL STEWART of B.B.C. fame
And presenting Every Week a Popular Guest Artiste ★
COMPLETE CHANGE OF PROGRAMME EVERY WEEK
s of Admission: Adults 5/- & 4/- Children 2/6 & 1/6
kets available in advance at Pavilion Booking Office. Open Daily 10 a.m. to 12 noon
and 1 p.m. Phone 2955.
.m. PAVILION CABARET 9 p.m.
BILL McCUE and MOIRA ANDERSON
invite you to meet them on
THURSDAY AT NINE
, Coffees and Light Refreshments on Sale. Admission 2/6

HARBOUR PAVILION, NORTH BERWICK
IDEAL FAMILY ENTERTAINMENT
THE WAGGLE OF THE KILT
IS CLANCY presenting
LIBBY STUART
Singing Star with Pep and Personality
with
PAUL CLANCY
Young Maestro of the Keyboards
JOHNNY ADAM
S.T.V. SHOWCASE COMEDY STAR
MAUREEN COLEMAN
'Solo Dancer'
RADIO AND CORDING STAR
Y WILSON
ordion 'Ace'
at 7.30 p.m.
JULY 5th, 12th, 19th, 26th, AUGUST 2nd, 9th.
on TUESDAYS
HOLIDAY SHOWTIME
presenting
JOE GORDON
ALLY LOGAN
Scotland's Top Duo Stars of S.T.V.
Grampian and B.B.C.
with
DANNY McCOLL
'A broth of a boy'
BERT SHORTHOUSE
'Scotland's Accordion Virtuoso'
IAN FRASER
The Young Versatile Mr Music
GORDON DANCERS
at 7.30 p.m.
JULY 7th, 14th, 21st, 28th

e a superb evening's
entertainment with
BILL & RAY
THE TARTAN LADS
With Comedian Compere
JACK MARTIN
The beautiful singing voice of
MAJELLA
and
Maureen and Morag
THE KIRBY DANCERS
Tickets £1.50. Senior Citizens, Children and Unemployed £1.00
arbour Pavilion, North Berwick
uesdays, July 6, 13, 20, 27, ugust 3 and 10
at 7.30 pm
Victoria Ballroom, Dunbar
Thursdays, July 8, 15, 22, 29, August 5 and 12
at 7.30 pm
Tourist Information Centre
NORTH BERWICK. Tel. 2197
Tickets in advance from:
Tourist Information Centre
DUNBAR. Tel. 63353

Pony Rides

With Town Council approval, Thomas Moncur started hiring donkeys and ponies on the East Beach in 1936. Moncur, from the Belford Riding Academy, Edinburgh came to North Berwick in 1929 when he took over David Runciman's riding business at the rear of the Commercial Hotel (now the County). Moncur was constrained to the beach between the foot of School Road and the Quadrant, to pay a rent of £2 for the season, and insure against likely claims, undertaking to relieve the Council of all claims brought against them in connection with the use of the beach by him.

Above : There were always willing helpers to assist Moncur. Here a local boy, with his takings satchel hanging at his side, leads a pony and happy rider along the beach. 1936

Left and below : As well as hiring donkeys and ponies on the beach, Moncur also took riders on escorted trips around the town.

Canoes for hire

Canoes became available for hire following John Marshall's application to the Town Council in the autumn of 1935. The following summer Marshall, from North Queensferry, started hiring his homemade canoes - canvas stiffened and water-proofed with dope over a wooden carcass - from the West Beach. A couple of seasons later Jackie Gordon took over the hiring business with 1939 being the last season they were available. Above : A heavy overcast day with the west bay like a mill pond - ideal for beginners trying out canoes. c1938

Flying Boats

FLYING BOAT AT NORTH BERWICK : LADY HAY TAKING HER TICKET

During August 1932 British Flying Boats Limited were given permission by North Berwick Burgh Council to land their flying boats off the harbour over five or six days. Lord Malcolm Douglas Hamilton, a director of the company, is seen consulting with James Brown, assistant Harbour Master, as to the best spots to land the flying boat "Cloud of Iona" to collect and deliver their passengers. Many prospective customers happily queued on the West Beach to buy their ticket including Lady Hay wife of Sir Duncan Hay, Bart.

LORD MALCOLM DOUGLAS HAMILTON CONSULTING JAMES BROWN

Above : Press cutting from August 10th 1932

Seaside Mission

The Church of Scotland, in its efforts to reach people with the Gospel, launched its programme of Seaside Missions in 1934 with the first two missions held in North Berwick and Leven, Fife. The aim of the missions was to try and reach the many people who were away from home on holiday, and the local residents.

Prior to this the Scripture Union ran a mission at Point Garry in the 1920s. Named the Children's Special Service Mission, it was usually conducted by Mr J. Stewart, a well-known missionary at the time. And earlier still, weekly open-air services at Point Garry had been a regular feature during the season from as early as 1892.

Prior to the war, missions were led for a month by a minister assisted by a divinity student. In 1934, the first seaside mission in North Berwick was led by the Rev. Grant Fleming and assisted by Bill Macartney and in 1935 the mission was led by Rev. McKenzie Grieve assisted by Tom Torrance. McKenzie Grieve continued to lead the seaside missions at North Berwick until the outbreak of war.

Services were held, weather permitting, on the sands and during inclement weather in a church hall. Often large crowds of children and adults attended. Games and various activities were organised for the children with services for older people in the evenings.

One of the more popular events organised by the mission was the tide fights. Groups of children would compete against each other building large sandcastles on the West

Rev. Grant Fleming (above) asks for attention, while his assistant, divinity student, Bill Macartney (top left) entertains pupils from the Guthrie School. 1934
Left : Rev. McKenzie Grieve. 1930s
Below : Grant Fleming, colleagues, and hundreds of children enjoy a glorious day at Seaside Mission. 1935

For the children of many locals and visitors the Seaside Mission in the 1930s was a wonderfully happy place to pass their summer holiday - having fun, playing games, learning about the gospel, and making new friends.

157

Beach. Topped with seaweed and other seaside detritus the winners were the group with the last castle standing against the incoming tide. An alternative version was when the entire troupe of children dug like crazy to build a barrier along the beach to prevent the tide coming in!

Following the success at North Berwick and Leven, other missions followed in other coastal towns like Girvan and Troon, and all continued each summer until World War 2, when they were suspended.

After the war, the seaside mission at North Berwick moved to the East Beach, and was lead sometimes by a minister or sometimes by a student leader. They would be accompanied by a team of young, and sometimes not so young, people with many coming from the west coast and sometimes as far as Aberdeen. With teams of generally young people taking part, it was easier to contact and relate to other young people in the centre where missions were held.

From Monday to Friday the day revolved around children's games and activities on the beach in the mornings. The afternoon started with a service followed by singing choruses, or perhaps a bible story or even a small play. Evenings saw the teenagers climbing the law or having sausage sizzles along at Jacob's Ladder or entertaining parents with plays like 'Mock Wedding'. Saturday was a day off followed by a normal Sunday with morning and evening services.

By the 1960s the mission could consist of as many as 24 young people from all walks of life who all gave up their holidays to come and help the church - sleeping in church halls and paying all their own expenses. In 1961 they were led by the Rev. Peter Bisset, of Rutherglen Church, Glasgow with the team divided up so that a section dealt with young children,

Tide fights were one of the most exciting activities organised during a Seaside Mission day with groups - often boys versus girls - competing to hold back the inevitable. 1930s

Above : Newly arrived for two weeks' holiday at North Berwick, over twenty volunteers from as far as Aberdeen and Glasgow, gladly giving up their time to help at Summer Mission. 1951

Top right : Sausage sizzle at the bottom of Jacob's ladder. 1952

Below right : Saturday night entertainment at the Blackadder Church Hall. A performance of 'A Mock Wedding'. 1951

Below : Volunteers and a few young thespians take time out to have their photograph taken. 1951

another with teenagers and the rest with the grown-ups. The mission reached out to the whole family and as a result, many people living or holidaying in these holiday resorts like North Berwick, started their journey of faith in Christianity through attending these missions.

In the 1970s, despite changes beginning to take place in society - with many more people starting to holiday abroad – the Mission team still visited North Berwick for a fortnight in August. The team, led by the Rev. Douglas Nicol from Crieff, started their day activities at 7.45am which included children's games, Christian literature distribution, barbecues and a youth café.

As the decade progressed and the exodus of Scottish tourists abroad increased there was not the same concentration on missions in some of the traditional seaside holiday resorts, although missions do still take place in many of these locations. At the same time there were increasing requests for missions to take place in inland parishes. Hence, the Church of Scotland changed the name from Seaside Mission to Summer Mission. Despite the exodus to foreign climes, in 1984 the Summer Mission celebrated 50 years in North Berwick marking the occasion with services, hymn singing and sausage sizzles on the East Beach.

Below : Celebrating 50 years of Summer Mission at North Berwick. 1984
Right : Press cutting from 'Evening Dispatch' July 1961.

Off to Church - on the sands

They were on the beach at North Berwick. Nearly 100 excited, singing kids looking up at a man on top of the sand castle with a microphone in his hands.

Nothing extraordinary in that you may say? Oh, but there was. They were at church - and at three in the afternoon on a week-day.

It was all part of a Church of Scotland plan for taking the gospel to the holiday crowds and taking the seriousness out of it for the children by introducing light-hearted hymn singing.

The mission at North Berwick consists of 24 young people from all walks of life. They gave up their holidays to come and help the church.

In other seaside resorts – Leven, Troon, Aberdeen, Girvan, among them – some 250 – 300 other young people do the same thing.

They sleep in church halls; pay all their own expenses, doing for themselves.

Led by the young Rev. Peter Bisset, of Rutherford Church, Glasgow, the team is divided up so that a section deals with the young children, another with teenagers, the rest with grown-ups.

"There is a job for everybody to do," the fair, wavy-haired minister told Picture Report.

From Glasgow came young Margaret Matheson, an electronics research engineer. She had given up her three weeks holiday to help at various social activities.

"I spent a week at Guide Camp, a week at a convention at Keswick, and a week here." She told Picture Report.

It all pays off, this personal evangelism. "Our teams see what their own faith means to them when they are helping others," said Mr Bisset.

The seaside church can report – "Mission accomplished."

Chip Shops

Popular for over a century and a half, chip shops across the country have provided a staple ready meal of fish and chips at reasonable cost to all manner of customers. For those around before the last war in North Berwick Maggie Gullane was synonymous with chips, and for those who could afford it, fish suppers. In her little 'chippie' in Forth Street, the cauldron of dripping always appeared to be boiling with chips. She had a big brown table with two long forms where, if weather was bad, you could sit and eat your chips. It was popular with the young who might buy a poke of chips with a 1d worth of beetroot if their pocket money stretched. For older customers it was a welcome stop for a fish or black pudding supper on the way home after a few drinks. Others would pop in for sustenance on the way down to the 'Piv' for a jig and a 'squeeze'.

Along in Quality Street, Jenny Elliot ran a similar equally popular establishment in the 1930s and early 40s. Taken over by Andrew Tomasi just after the War, the chip shop business has been run by various members of the Cucchi family since 1970. Popular with tourists, returning visitors happily queue for a fish supper after a leisurely day on the beach. And going in to 'N.B. Fry' is like visiting old friends - being greeted by the same faces, year after year.

Right : Maggie Gullane, proprietrix of her eponymous chipshop. 1930s
Below centre : Jenny Elliot (second right) and her staff. 1938
Below left : North Berwick Fry - for visitors, sitting-in, is like having tea with old friends. 2013

Walking Snaps

Between the Wars it was popular for photographers to visit the town during the summer months and take photographs of pedestrians as they approached them, often catching the pedestrians unawares. The Town Council frequently received applications from firms such as J. D. Ewart Ltd, Empire Films and Scotia Films for one of their operators to come to North Berwick during the season to take 'walking snaps'. In return for their request for the sole right of taking 'movie snaps' as they were sometimes called, the firm would offer the Council a small fee of a few pounds. In all cases the applicant was informed that their operator would be welcome but their request for sole rights were always declined and the Council always suggested that a donation to the funds for the Edington Convalescent Home would be very much appreciated.

Favourite spots for taking the photographs were Harbour Terrace and the High Street - between the Oak Café (now an Indian restaurant) and the Abbey Church. The photographer would issue a ticket/receipt to the pedestrian(s) after the photo had been taken. Prior to this the photographer would have made arrangements with a local shop to have the photographs available for viewing by the pedestrian – probably the following day. If the pedestrian liked the image it could be purchased for a few coppers (pence).

North Berwick Scouts' Aquatic Carnival - 25th July 1936

One of the brightest and most amusing events of the 1936 summer season was the aquatic carnival held in the swimming pond by the North Berwick Scout Group. The scouts, who were celebrating their 28th anniversary that same week, were joined by the Girl Guides, Scouts from Coatbrdge, Airdrie, Craiglockhart, Wishaw and Dumbarton, and the 55th and 198th Glasgow Companies of Boys' Brigade. The carnival was composed almost entirely of novelty and humorous events including an aquatic recreation of the 1936 Derby; a display by the North Berwick section of the Women's League of Health and Beauty performed by the Scouts; an attempt, by Rover-mate Jack Stewart, to swim a length of the pond with a 56lb weight on his chest; and an underwater race involving the discarding of certain items of clothing. All funds raised over the course of the afternoon were collected for the benefit of the Edinburgh Royal Infirmary.

NORTH BERWICK SCOUT GROUP

HOT-CHA
AQUATIC CARNIVAL

IN THE

North Berwick Swimming Pond

IN AID OF

EDINBURGH ROYAL INFIRMARY

On JULY 25th, at 3.15 p.m.

SNAPPIEST
SILLIEST
STUPIDEST

SWIFTEST, SALT SEA SWIMMING EVER STAGED

Roll up and See North Berwick's Funniest Gala and

HELP THE INFIRMARY

ADMISSION ONE SHILLING

Printed at The White House, North Berwick

East Lothian Boy Scouts Association

North   Scout
Berwick   Group

Aquatic Carnival

IN

Swimming Pond, North Berwick

ON

SATURDAY, 25th JULY 1936

Due to commence at 3.15 p.m.

In aid of
Edinburgh Royal Infirmary

Programme One Penny at least

PROGRAMME

1. **The Balloon Goes Up**

2. **50 Yards Cub Handicap Race**

	Secs.	Go at		Secs.	Go at
B. Crockett	scr.	8	R. Reid	1	7
L. Blaney	1	7	H. Young	3	5
F. Coventry	2	6	G. Young	3	Go

3. **Women's League of Health and Beauty**
   (North Berwick Section)
   Led by Miss Patricia Winterbottom

4. **Team Race**

	Secs.	Go at
Coatbridge Scouts	scr.	60
198th Glasgow B.B.	6	54
138th Craiglockhart Scouts	10	50
North Berwick Scouts	10	50
55th Glasgow B.B.	60	Go

5. **The Gold Rush**
   (Get your spare change ready its all to help the E.R.I.)

6. **Novelty Diving**

7. **Our Big Challenge**
   Rover Mate J. A. STEWART will attempt the almost impossible feat of swimming with a 56-lb. weight on his chest.

8. **North Berwick Girl Guides** (Bacon & Egg Race)

9. **Diving Display**

---

10. **Underwater Race** (Open to Boys Brigade and Scouts)

11. **50 Yards Scout Handicap Race**

1st HEAT	Secs.	Go at	2nd HEAT	Secs.	Go at
W. Stewart, 138th Craiglockhart	scr.	18	W. Aitken, N. Ber'k	scr.	18
J. Veitch, Y.M.C.A.	1	17	J. Brown, 9th Coatb'ge	1	17
A. Macpherson, 138th Craiglockhart	1	17	J. Martin, Airdrie	2	16
R. Smith, 138th Craiglockhart	1	17	J. Gagen, 138th Craiglockhart	5	13
J. Rae, 9th Coatbridge	1	17	J. Riddle, 138th Craiglockhart	10	8
W. Rollo, N. Berwick	3	15	J. Livingstone, N. B'k	10	8
H. Craig, 9th Coatb'ge	4	14	J. Clifford, 4th D'bart'n	10	8
J. Torrance, 4th W'h'w	16	2	J. Walker, 4th Wishaw	13	5

   First, Second and Third in each heat to swim in Final

12. **Pairs Life Saving Race**
   (Open to The Boys Brigade and Scouts)

13. **Undressing Race**

14. **Final of Event 11**

15. **Presentation of Prizes by**
   Capt. A. G. Spence, Scottish Headquarters Commissioner

16. **The Derby 1936**

FINIS
(And You are late for Tea)

SCOUTING NEWS.

The Scout Movement, which Lord Baden Powell started in England in 1908, is now World Wide. There are now Official Scouts attached through Imperial Headquarters, London, in 49 different countries, with a total strength of considerably over 2,250,000.

NORTH BERWICK SCOUTS were amongst the first to start in Scotland, the Troop being inaugurated in August 1908.

A World Jamboree is to be held in Holland next summer, when Boy Scouts from the four corners of the Earth will gather together to foster international goodwill and fellowship; Great Britain will send a contingent of about 6,000,—1,000 of these will come from Scotland.

For the uninitiated a Scout Group consists of a Rover Crew, Scout Troop, and Cub Pack. At the last census the North Berwick Group was over 110 strong. The Troop have just returned from a most successful camp on the Banks of Lake Windermere, while individual Rovers have been enjoying Camping and Hiking in various parts of Scotland, one member of the Crew at present being on a Cycle Tour in Germany.

During the afternoon we hope to play you some selections from our Record Breaking Pantomime which was run in aid of the Royal Infirmary last Xmas, in the North Berwick Pavilion.

COMING EVENTS AT THE POND.

8th August	JIMMY RAE & HANK AKERS, The famous Acrobatic Divers.
15th August	GALA.
26th August	ILLUMINATED CARNIVAL NIGHT.
26 to 28 Aug.	PETE DESJARDINS, U.S.A. The little bronze statue from Florida.
27th August	CHILDREN'S GALA—Pupils taught at Pond.
9th Sept.	HAROLD "DUTCH" SMITH, U.S.A. Diving Champion of the World. AND ILLUMINATED WATER CARNIVAL.

Messin' About

For many young children the opportunity to get into a boat, whether it was on the water, lying on the beach or in the harbour, provided a great opportunity for them to test their skills and act out their fantasies. It gave the 'Captain' the opportunity the sail the 'Seven Seas' and the pirate the chance to plunder treasure in far-off tropical seas. For all, when near or on water, the sternest test was always making sure you stayed dry. Returning to naval H.Q., where mother awaited, soaked to the skin was never a good idea.

This lively crew in the 1930s look ready to cast-off to some cold, far-off land. Not too far as there appears to be a shortage of provisions aboard and they may have to wait for an incoming tide to launch.

Above : 'Steady as she goes' - this young sailor looks a little concerned as to the speed he may be pushed off at. c1931

Above-Right and Right : Two 'able-seamen' aboard the 'Britannia' awaiting passengers for a sight-seeing voyage to the furthest edges of the Firth of Forth to see the Bass Rock and its gannets. c1956

The Playhouse

The Playhouse was, for almost fifty years a very popular venue with people of all ages, both local and visitor. Opened on the 7th July 1938 the cinema was built on the site previously occupied by the Forrester's Hall, where Tommy Scott had, up to that time, shown films over a period of thirty years. Scott's business was eventually taken over by Caledonian Associated Cinemas Limited, and it was they who built the new 'art deco' building to house the cinema.

Saturday matinees were always popular with local children and many from Gullane and Dirleton were happy to walk in, saving their bus fare for more sweets. When the latest Western or Disney cartoon was first shown, queues could stretch all the way up to St Andrew Street. During poor summer weather, weekday matinees were put on for all children providing some relief for visiting parents.

COMING ATTRACTIONS

THE PLAYHOUSE
NORTH BERWICK

Complimentary Pass

This Pass is the prop
Playhouse Management
TRANSFERABLE.

Proprietors
Caledonian Associated
Inverness

1/-
Including Tax
1275

1/6   1/6
1410

Transfer 6
1/10 to 2/4
INCLUDING TAX

Craig Swim

Ned Barney, M. Stenhouse, Miss Vanda Baillie, the first three home in the inaugural 1948 Craig Swim.

Since the turn of the century sea-swims have often featured during the summer months. Swims from Craigleith became almost regular events by the twenties with pond-master Jim McCracken often taking pupils out to the island for them to swim back. A three-mile Bass Rock swim was for serious swimmers only with the challenge often attracting cross channel and olympic swimmers. Greased-up, the swimmers had to battle with currents, tides and extreme cold – whatever the season.

On the evening of 27 August 1948 a new aquatic event was inaugurated by North Berwick Swimming Club when the first formal competitive swim from the island of Craigleith took place. Ten competitors took part in the three-quarter mile event that was won by W. E. 'Ned' Barnie, the well-known Portobello long-distance swimmer. The race from the island to the beach on the West Bay was won in a time of 35 minutes 52 seconds. Weather was perfect and the race was witnessed by hundreds

A precursor to the Craig Swim was the North Berwick Long-Distance Swim which was often held during the twenties and thirties. Held between the 'Old Pier' and the Harbour, the handicap event attracted quite a number of competitors and was very popular among the members of the local swimming club. This magazine photograph shows winner Miss Geraldine Thomson, Castleton, being held high by her fellow competitors. c1937

Top Left : Competitors for the 1968 Craig Swim.
Bottom Left : Winner of the 1968 Craig Swim Alistair McGregor of Warrender B.C. being presented with the trophy by William Turner, President of the North Berwick Swimming Club.
Right : Certificate presented to twelve year-old Alison Scott after her successful 1970 Craig Swim.

NORTH BERWICK AMATEUR SWIMMING CLUB
'CRAIG' OPEN SEA SWIM
This is to certify that A. SCOTT competed in the Annual Open Sea Swim from 'Craigleith' to the Old Pier, North Berwick, and returned the time of 29 minutes 30 seconds.
24 Aug 1970   Signed William Levine
PRESIDENT

of spectators on the shore. A cup was donated by "a number of sporting gentlemen" and was presented to the winner by Provost George Gilbert. Taking second place was M. Stenhouse, Warrender B.C. and third was local teenager Vanda Baillie representing North Berwick Swimming Club.

Later, in the 1960s, the race was still an important event in the summer calendar. The 1968 race – then from Craigleith to the old pier - attracted fifteen entries and was won by Alistair McGregor, of Warrender Swimming Club, in a record time of 14 minutes 54 seconds. All competitors finished the course with Alistair Stewart, the first local, in a time of 22 minutes 45 seconds and the youngest, ten year-old local school girl Alison Scott, finishing in a time of 33 minutes.

Law Race

During a week of festivities held to celebrate the Coronation of Queen Elizabeth in 1953, the first Law Race was held. Starting at Struth's butcher shop, the route went straight up Law Road to the bottom of the Law then straight up to the top where successful runners were presented with a sash. Then it was back down to the bottom, down Law Road then right along Kirk Ports to the Lodge where prizes were presented to the winners. Sandy Young, a twenty-four year old local was first across the line in a time of 16 minutes and 16 seconds and was presented with a cup by Mr Strudwick. Since 1953 the challenge of the Law Race has been taken-up by thousands of runners and by 2012 had been run 46 times. Over its history the course of the race has changed numerous times. Today it starts and finishes at the harbour and the number of entries has grown - averaging over two hundred in recent years – with competitors both local and from Edinburgh and the south-east of Scotland. The fastest men complete the course in under 18 minutes with the fastest ladies taking just over 20 minutes.

Above : Sandy Young receiving his winner's cup from Baillie Strudwick after winning the first Law Race. 1953
Right : Council posters from 2002 and 1958

170

What's Going On?

To ensure the widest publicity for the summer season N.B. Town Council prepared bill posters early in the year. They listed all forthcoming events and were placed around the town and also into local county publications. In addition, many of the more popular events were publicised by their own hand bills too.

East Putting Course

A MIXED FOURSOMES
PUTTING COMPETITION
OPEN TO ALL AMATEURS

WILL BE HELD OVER THIS COURSE

On TUESDAY and WEDNESDAY, 19th and 20th JULY

Qualifying rounds will be played on the 19th July commencing at 2 p.m. No cards will be issued after 8 p.m. Entrants may play one or more rounds to qualify. A draw will be made from the players (1st 16 Ladies and 1st 16 Gentlemen) with lowest stroke scores and they will play off by match play on the 20th July commencing at 6 p.m.

Prizes will be given for best qualifying round by Lady and Gentleman and to the Finalists and Semi-Finalists.

ENTRY MONEY, 6d. per Round in the Qualifying Stage

North Berwick
JULY 1957

J. WALLACE MENZIES
Town Clerk

ROYAL BURGH OF NORTH BERWICK

Competitions 6th - 16th JULY 1959

PUTTING

Monday, 6th July, East Course, Visitors only

Qualifying Rounds by stroke play will be played commencing 10 a.m. No cards will be issued after 12 noon. Entrants may play one or more rounds to qualify, lowest score to count. In the event of ties, the score for the first nine holes to decide. The 16 players (1st 8 ladies and 1st 8 gentlemen) with lowest stroke scores to play off by match play at 2 p.m. Prizes will be given to Finalists and Semi-Finalists. Entry 6d. per round in qualifying stage.

Monday, 13th July — West Course

CHILDREN UNDER 14 YEARS OF AGE

The same times and regulations governing the putting competition on 6th July will apply except that the qualifiers will be 8 and no distinction will be made between boys and girls.

YACHT Competition and Exhibition

Thursday, 9th July at the Yacht Pond

At 11 a.m. Entries will be taken at the Yacht Pond from 10.30 a.m. Prizes will be given to the owners of yachts of residents and visitors competing in the following classes:
1. For best models in each class. 2. For fastest in each class. 3. For mechanically propelled yachts.

FISHING

Thursday, 16th July at the Harbour

This competition for children under 14 years of age will be held at the Harbour where places will be allocated at 10.30 a.m. The competition will last for one hour and prizes will be presented. Competitors will require to provide their own tackle and bait.

SAND MODELLING

Wednesday, 15th July on West Beach

Areas will be allocated to each competitor and will be available at 2.30 p.m. The models will be judged at 3.30 p.m. Each model must be formed solely from materials available on the shore.
Prizes will be given in the following classes: 1. Up to 7 years. 2. 7 to 10 years. 3. 10 to 12 years. 4. 12 to 14 years.

WILLIAM SIMPSON, Town Chamberlain

ROYAL BURGH OF NORTH BERWICK

EVENTS TO BE HELD DURING SEASON 1949

YACHT RACING every Thursday at 6.30 p.m. and every Saturday at 3 p.m. during June, July, August and September

JUNE	9th (Thursday)	PUTTING COMPETITION on the West Putting Course.
,,	23rd (Thursday)	PUTTING COMPETITION on the East Putting Course.
,,	25th (Saturday)	SWIMMING GALA.
,,	25th (Saturday)	COLTNESS WORKS SILVER BAND.
JULY	5th (Tuesday)	YACHT COMPETITION FOR CHILDREN in the Yacht Pond.
,,	6th (Wednesday)	PUTTING COMPETITION on the West Putting Course.
,,	9th (Saturday)	SWIMMING GALA.
,,	13th (Wednesday)	EVENING SWIMMING GALA.
,,	14th (Thursday)	SAND COMPETITION FOR CHILDREN on West Bay.
,,	14th (Thursday)	GYMKHANA in "Lady Jane" Park.
,,	21st (Thursday)	SHEEP DOG TRIALS in "Lady Jane" Park.
,,	20th to 24th	SCOTTISH AMATEUR GOLF CHAMPIONSHIP—MATCH PLAY (On Muirfield)
,,	22nd (Friday)	PUTTING COMPETITION (Visitors Only) on East Putting Course.
AUG.	4th (Thursday)	PUTTING COMPETITION (Qualifying) CALDER CUP on West Putting Course.
,,	5th (Friday)	MATCH PLAY—CALDER CUP on West Putting Course.
,,	6th (Saturday)	SWIMMING GALA.
,,	6th (Saturday)	CLYDEBANK BURGH BAND.
,,	8th (Monday)	TENNIS TOURNAMENT—Starts.
,,	13th (Saturday)	TENNIS TOURNAMENT—Ends.
,,	13th (Saturday)	FINAL OF ESMOND TROPHY on Burgh Golf Course.
,,	16th (Tuesday)	SAND COMPETITION FOR CHILDREN on West Bay.
,,	17th (Wednesday)	YACHT COMPETITION FOR CHILDREN in Yacht Pond.
,,	18th (Thursday)	GARDEN FETE in Lodge Grounds.
,,	18th (Thursday)	SWIMMING GALA FOR CHILDREN.
,,	20th (Saturday)	REGATTA.
,,	23rd (Tuesday)	PUTTING COMPETITION (Visitors) on East Putting Course.
,,	25th (Thursday)	EVENING SWIMMING GALA.
,,	27th (Saturday)	COL. WEIR ROSE BOWL (Handicap) and MISS COUPER CUP (Scratch) FOR LADIES on Burgh Golf Course.
,,	27th (Saturday)	HALDANE CUP (Open Handicap for Men) on Burgh Golf Course.
SEPT.	6th (Tuesday)	PUTTING COMPETITION on West Putting Course.
,,	8th (Thursday)	EVENING SWIMMING GALA.
,,	10th (Saturday)	PUTTING COMPETITION on East Putting Course.

FOR FURTHER INFORMATION SEE SEPARATE POSTERS PUBLISHED FOR EACH EVENT

Royal Burgh of North Berwick

LIST OF EVENTS
SEASON 1962

APRIL	16-21	Mon. to Sat.	Scottish Boys' Golf Championship on West Links.
	19-20	Thurs./Fri.	David Blair Putter Tournament for Boys on Burgh and West Links.
MAY	12	Saturday	Edinburgh to North Berwick Marathon Race.
JUNE	2	Saturday	Opening of the Swimming Pond.
	2	Saturday	Eglinton Quaich—Stableford Mixed Foursomes (Handicap) on West Links.
	4-8	Mon. to Fri.	Open Championship of the Society of One Armed Golfers on West Links.
	16-17	Sat./Sun.	Scottish Dinghy Association Single Handed Championship.
	21 and 23	Thurs. and Sat.	Cecilia Gilholm Putting Trophy qualifying rounds on East Putting Course.
	28	Thursday	Cecilia Gilholm Putting Trophy Match Play.
	30	Saturday	North Berwick Swimming Club Gala.
JULY	3	Tuesday	Model Yacht Competition at Yacht Pond.
	4	Wednesday	Putting Competition for Visitors on West Putting Course.
	5	Thursday	Evening Dispatch Bathing Beauty Competition and Children's Events.
	7	Saturday	North Berwick Rugby Club Garden Fete.
	9	Monday	Aqua Antics at the Swimming Pond.
	12	Thursday	Sand Modelling Competition on West Beach.
			Children's Fishing Competition at Harbour.
	14	Saturday	Royal Burgh Regatta (E.L.Y.C.).
			R.N. Lifeboat Day. Dunbar Lifeboat visits North Berwick.
	15	Sunday	Royal Burgh Regatta continued.
	16	Monday	North Berwick Rugby Club Dance on Esplanade.
	17	Tuesday	American Tournament on Burgh Tennis Courts.
			Model Yacht Competition at Yacht Pond.
	18	Wednesday	Children's Putting Competition on West Putting Course.
	19	Thursday	Community Association Fete and Fun Fair at Pavilion.
			Race to top of Law.
	20	Friday	Putting Competition for Visitors on East Putting Course.
	21	Saturday	Esmond Golf Trophy Qualifying on West Links.
			Roman Catholic Church Garden Fete.
			East Lothian County Jubilee Cup Competition on Bowling Green.
	22	Sunday	North Berwick Rugby Club Car Treasure Hunt.
	23	Monday	Aqua Antics at the Swimming Pond.
			Community Association Dance on Esplanade.
	24	Tuesday	Sand Modelling Competition on West Beach.
	26	Thursday	Evening Dispatch Bathing Beauty Competition and Children's Events.
			Children's Fishing Competition at Harbour.
AUGUST	3	Friday	Putting Competition for Visitors on East Putting Course.
	4	Saturday	Esmond Golf Trophy Final on West Links.
			North Berwick Boy Scouts Garden Fete.
	6	Monday	Aqua Antics at Swimming Pond.
	7	Tuesday	Model Yacht Competition at Yacht Pond.
	8	Wednesday	Sand Modelling Competition on West Beach.
	9-10	Thurs./Fri.	Calder Cup Putting Competition on West Putting Course.
	10-11	Fri./Sat.	Scotland v. England Tennis International on Burgh Tennis Courts.
	11	Saturday	British Legion Garden Fete.
	13-18	Mon./Sat.	East Lothian Tennis Tournament on Burgh Tennis Courts.
	13	Monday	North Berwick Tennis Club Dance at Pavilion.
	14	Tuesday	Children's Fishing Competition at Harbour.
	16	Thursday	Children's Swimming Gala.
	17	Friday	Children's Putting Competition on East Putting Course.
	18	Saturday	Haldane Cup and Town Council Salver Competition for Gentlemen, on Burgh Course.
	19	Sunday	North Berwick Rugby Club Car Treasure Hunt.
	20	Monday	Aqua Antics at the Swimming Pond.
	21	Tuesday	Model Yacht Competition at Yacht Pond.
	22	Wednesday	Evening Dispatch Bathing Beauty Competition and Children's Events.
	23	Thursday	Open Putting Competition on West Putting Course.
	24	Friday	Sand Modelling Competition on West Beach.
	25	Saturday	Col. Weir Rosebowl and Miss Couper Cup for Ladies on Burgh Course.
			International Swimming Gala—Warrender Swimming Club v. Frieburg Swimming Club (South Germany).
			Scottish Bowling Association Council v. East Lothian Bowling Association on Bowling Green.
	28	Tuesday	Open Fishing Competition at Harbour.
SEPTEMBER	4	Tuesday	Open Putting Competition on East Putting Course.
	6	Thursday	Scottish Rock Garden Club Flower Show in Sun Shelter.
	12	Wednesday	Open Putting Competition on West Putting Course.
	13-15	Thurs./Sat.	North Berwick Open Mixed Foursomes on West Links.
	21	Friday	North Berwick Rugby Club Dance at Pavilion.
	29-30	Sat./Sun.	International Sea Angling Championship.

Pavilion Entertainments

VARIETY—Follies of 1962 Tuesday, Wednesday and Thursday at 8 p.m.
CHILDREN'S CORNER—Tuesday and Friday 6 p.m. - 7 p.m.
DANCING—Friday 9 p.m. - 1 a.m. Saturday 8.30 p.m. - 11.30 p.m.

Yachting

Racing every Thursday at 6.30 p.m. and on Saturdays during June, July, August and September.

Golf

Mixed Foursomes every Tuesday evening on Burgh Golf Course.

North Berwick Swimming Pond - The Post-War Years

Although the pond had been completely renovated in 1930 the water still had to be changed every 10 days or so as it got very dirty. To ensure the pond was out of action for the least possible time this operation took place overnight. In the evening after the pond closed, valves half way along the pond were opened which discharged water into the east end of the harbour, then the drain at the deep-end was opened which discharged pond-water directly into the sea. Once empty the pond was doused with Chloride of Lime and then the surface was scubbed by six men with 'Bass' brooms and deck scrubbers. The pond was then refilled with water pumped directly from the sea, with the whole operation taking twelve to fourteen hours depending upon tides. When it reopened it was not unusual for swimmers to complain about burning eyes, such was the precarious nature of the cleaning and nothing was measured.

AQUACABARET

to be held at

THE POND
NORTH BERWICK

Monday 17th September 1956

3.15 p.m.   Gates Open 2.30 p.m.

Daring Acrobatic Diving by

DREW KENNEDY   MIKE TROUP
R.A.F. Diving Champion 1952   Scotland's Funniest Comedy Diver

The TRAMPOMANIACS   The JERRY BUILDERS
Trampoline Act

THE GOONS
JOHN CAIRNS   DAVE McCONNELL   ALASDAIR LAIDLAW

One hour of riotous fun and thrills

Charges of Admission: Adults 2/= Children under 16 1/-

By the late 1950s the Medical Officer for Health thought that the process was haphazard, and being aware of the extra pollution that then existed in the sea, insisted the water be filtered and chlorinated. Rock was blasted and excavated below the sun shelter and a small chlorine plant installed. Then in 1964, following an approach from Scottish Gas, with its new supply of gas from the North Sea, a heat plant was installed and the pond was finally heated. To ensure all bathers were paying bathers – and not sneaking in after-hours - the pond area was enclosed with blue and amber Fillon plastic screens.

The early years after the Second World War continued to see well-attended galas with the pond-masters still taking responsibility for the content. By then it was more commonly called the 'pool', although it was still referred to in Council publicity material as the 'pond'. By the sixties there were fewer galas and the number of spectators attending had started to dwindle. 'Shivery bites', along with Brodie's pies were still available from a small kiosk but from the early 1970s, when tourists were starting to seek foreign climes, dwindling demand meant the end for refreshments.

From 1975, following the regionalisation of local government, the pool was run by East Lothian Council from Haddington, with the organisation and running of galas contracted out.

Previous Page : Opening ceremony for the 1963 season performed by Provost Johnny Fowler which was held, judging by the travel rug and winter coats, on a rather cold June afternoon.

Below : Much better weather for a well-attended Aqua Show & Beauty Contest with Drew Kennedy and his beautiful assistant going through part of their acrobatic act on the boom. c1960

Aqua Lovelies c1960

Five girls really in the swim are the chorus of "Nautical Nonsense', the professional aqua show run by pond-master Drew Kennedy. The girls danced on the boom before taking to the water to give a demonstration of precision swimming.

Gala Week

Gala Week and the crowning of the North Berwick Gala Queen were among the highlights of the summers from 1972 through to the beginning of the eighties. Organised by the Gala Committee, the week started on the second Saturday afternoon in July with the crowning in the Lodge Grounds of the Gala Queen. The Queen and her attending court were chosen by the pupils of Law Primary School with the Queen crowned usually by the wife of a local dignitary. However, Peter Purves, the Blue Peter presenter, performed the crowning in 1976 and Russell Hunter star of TV, radio and theatre did the honours in 1979. The crown and mace, both made from leather, were designed and crafted by local man, Robert Thom.

The ceremony was followed by children's sports and games along with musical entertainment provided by the North Berwick Pipe Band. Displays of judo and highland dancing were often held, as well as games for adults: tug of war, wellie boot throwing, pitch and putt, beat the goalie and the Bonnie Baby Contest.

After refreshments when children were presented with picnic bags, entrants for the fancy dress parade would assemble to be judged, followed by the awarding of prizes by the Gala Queen. There then followed a tour of the town by the Queen and her court, and the fancy dress entrants on decorated floats led by the fire brigade, Blue Peter Lifeboat and the pipe band.

Over the course of the following week, the diary was filled with events for all ages: junior discos, swimming galas and pet shows for the children; street fair and party, arts and crafts exhibitions, whist and dominoes, and a grand gala dinner dance for the adults. There was also five-a-side and crazy football, netball, and a golf tournament for the sporty with events for the athletic including a 'round the burgh' race, 'housewives race' and 'round the pubs' race.

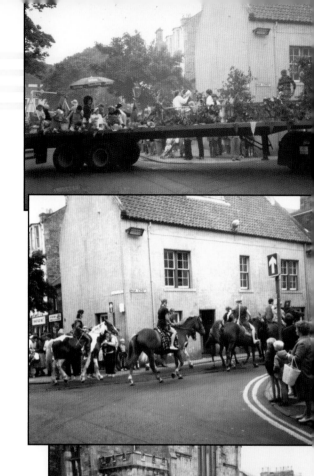

Page opposite : Following an eventful afternoon in the Lodge which started with the crowning of the Gala Queen and continued with the many children's sports and competitions, a parade of decorated floats toured the main streets of the town. Led by the North Berwick Pipe Band, the Lifeboat and a float with the Queen and her Court, the parade included vintage vehicles, military bands and the many decorated floats sponsored by local businesses.

Clockwise from top left : Gala Queens and their courts, Gillian Kirkpatrick 1980, Gillian Hughes 1978, Deborah Murray 1977, Susan Huish 1979, Lorna Hall 1975, Gillian Pert 1974, Maria Iannerilli 1976.

Fund-raising included various challenges - Bunny Bingo and Pitch and Putt. For the professional photographer there was no shortage of volunteers happy to oblige with a pose.

Tartan Fairs

The 'Tartan Fair' held on an August Sunday afternoon in the Lodge Grounds, ran for almost thirty years from the early seventies through to the late nineties. Held in aid of funds for the North Berwick Pipe Band, the 'Fairs' took a huge effort by the band to organise but proved very successful both regarding the funds raised and also in the numbers attending.

The afternoon started with the crowds being entertained to a repertoire of tunes by a guest band - Monktonhall Colliery Pipe Band and the Musselburgh and Fisherrow Trades Brass Band were among the many who performed over the years. During the seventies the Gala Queen and her Court would visit, piped in by members of the local band.

The dog show was always very popular and usually saw a large number of entries, so competition was fierce to find the most obedient, the prettiest, and the most-like-their owner entrants, and for the younger members of the crowd they could compete in their own children's novelty dog show.

Another of the day's attractions was the feat of strength competitions with participants throwing everything from wellies, sheaves of corn, and even haggis. The tug-of-war also proved entertaining, as did 'Pelt the Piper' where the poor piper put his head in the pillory and allowed himself to be showered with porridge.

Dancers demonstrated their skill with an exhibition of Highland Dancing. Stalls, side-shows and teas provided amusement and refreshment throughout the afternoon and helped raise valuable funds for the local band. The afternoon finished with the local and visiting band playing together down at Quality Street.

Above : Members of North Berwick Pipe Band, dressed in their No. 1 dress uniform, preparing for a performance at the Recreation Park. 1970s
Below : Dancers practising before giving a demonstration of Highland Dancing at the 1984 Tartan Fair.

Fred Marr and 'Sula II'

On leaving school, during the Second War, Fred Marr joined his father, Alf, fishing for lobsters and crabs from the 'Nora', their small inshore fishing boat. Some years later during the summer season, Fred worked for David Tweedie on his motor launches eventually going on to skipper one.

In 1961 Fred commissioned the building of his own fishing boat from the Cockenzie boatyards. Fred used his boat, named 'Girl Pat' after his daughter, for both fishing, taking out fishing trips and ferrying small parties to the Bass Rock. By the late sixties, after Tweedie retired and sold his motor launches, Fred was the only operator offering trips to the islands from North Berwick.

By 1971 Fred was confident enough to purchase his first passenger boat, 'Sula', (derived from the scientific name for the gannet *sula bassana*) with which he started regular sailings to the Bass and Fidra during the months of April to September. 'Sula' was replaced a year later by 'Sula II', with Fred and his son, Chris, running both boats for the 1972 season, before disposing of 'Sula'.

Previously called 'Janet', her former owner used to fish long shore herring nets with her in winter months during which she was fitted with a covered area at the bow end to give shelter and protection during wild winter days. She was a magnificent 41 foot launch built in 1965 by Eastick Yacht Station at Acle on the Norfolk Broads. Clinker-built out of Honduras mahogany she could carry, once a new lifeboat was fitted, 67 passengers and two crew and had a service speed of 7.5 knots.

As well as taking out passengers to the Bass, Fred and Chris provided the main mode of transport to the Bass for the Northern Lighthouse Board (NLB) - delivering mail, provisions and replacement keepers, before the helipad was built. Other than the NLB, the Marrs eventually became the only people permitted to land passengers on the Bass Rock, when Sir

Above : Two 'worthies' of the town, Chris and Fred Marr. c1973
Below : 'Sula II' en route to Bass Rock with a boat-load of passengers. c1976
Page opposite : (top centre) Prince Charles aboard 'Sula II' at the Bass Rock with other members of the opening party for the Scottish Seabird Centre. 2000

Hew Hamilton Dalrymple recognised that Fred was a natural conservationist and well-able to assist in the control and welfare of the gannet colony. Fred travelled to the Bass Rock every year taking bird-watchers, photographers and day-trippers from April to September and also through the winter months, as and when required by the NLB, up until the automation of the light in 1988.

As well as doing his bit for tourism, Fred was a great servant to the world of conservation and the environment. Part of this work was the rescuing of chicks which had either fallen from their nests or been abandoned by parents. Rather than see them starve or drown, Fred picked them up and hand reared them at the bottom of his garden until they were fully-fledged and ready to be released.

Fred freely gave of his time to deliver talks and slide shows on the Bass Rock and the local flora and fauna to various organisations, and with his knowledge and love of gannets and the Bass Rock, was able to impart this to a worldwide audience.

Fred skippered passenger boats from the harbour at North Berwick for over 50 years and retired in 2003 on his 80th birthday. For more than 30 years he delighted thousands of passengers with his scenic tours around the Bass Rock and Fidra with his own boat 'Sula II'. Chris and Pat continued enthralling passengers aboard 'Sula II' until their retirement in 2010 when the business was taken over by Forth Boat Tours.

Fred Marr died in 2008.

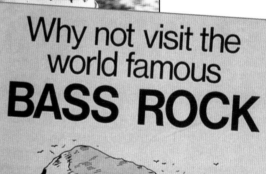
179

BBC's 'Its a Knockout'

'It's a Knockout' was a televised comedy game show popular in the 60s, 70s and 80s, and part of the *Jeux Sans Frontieres* franchise. It featured teams from across the country that would compete, one against another, with the winners entering the next round representing the UK against continental opposition. Games invariably involved water with players trying to either cross water or being squirted with water cannons by opposing teams. Foam was another ingredient as were daft, oversized costumes which were designed to inconvenience the wearer and provide maximum entertainment to those watching. Competition was fierce with each team training for months before the event, each eager to advance to the next round. It was all harmless slapstick which made for an entertaining and amusing evening entertainment on the BBC.

North Berwick competed in Heat 3 of the 1973 series of 'It's a Knockout' taking on Peebles. Team captain was John McAlpine, PE teacher at North Berwick High School, and head coach was Eric Smith, Pond-master at the pool. Training involved endurance running at the school playing fields and circuit training in the school gymnasium. Once the BBC released the games to be played during the actual event, they were simulated at Newbattle Baths where North Berwick went to train.

The match held on Sunday 6th May 1973 was a sell-out with all seats at 50p each, and all standing room at 25p. An estimated audience of 2000 watched the spectacle. Both teams, each supported by their own cheer leaders, were confident of victory with the winner travelling to the south of France two months later. The match, made up of seven games and a marathon finale, started well for North Berwick when it won the first game to lead 2 - 0. Sadly, from that point it all went badly for the home team and Peebles won the next five games to lead 10 – 2. The last game was won by the home side playing their joker and brought a little respectability to their score at 10 – 6 but unfortunately they went on to lose the marathon and the match 16 – 6.

After the match, both sides were entertained to a buffet reception at the Marine Hotel courtesy of the North Berwick Town Council.

Left - Team member badge
Right - Match Programme

THE B.B.C. PRESENTS

IT'S A

KNOCKOUT

NORTH BERWICK
v
PEEBLES

North Berwick Pool

May 6th 1973

Game 1 - Box Stacking

Game 2 - See-Saw Balance

*Right - North Berwick
Team and Cheer Leaders*

Game 3 - Bicycle Race

Game 5 - Rope Swing

Game 7 - Tub Race

Game 4 - Ball Crossing

Game 6 - Jumping Waiters

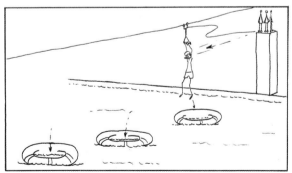

Marathon - Wire Slide

Raft Race

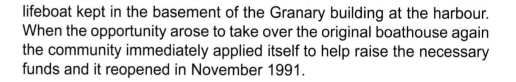

Following a suggestion by Ronnie Coates-Walker, Honorary Secretary for the local lifeboat Station, to hold a raft race and fair on the West Beach as a means of raising funds for the lifeboat and the refurbishment of the original boathouse, the first event was held in 1988.

Since the closing of the North Berwick Lifeboat Station in 1925, the lifeboat house had been used as a café for over seventy years – firstly as George Thomson's 'LB' or 'Lifeboat Café', then as the 'Café Anglais' of the Capaldi family, and finally the 'Victoria Café' by the Iannerilli family, known locally as 'Mario's'.

With the arrival of Blue Peter III in 1966 the Station reopened with the

lifeboat kept in the basement of the Granary building at the harbour. When the opportunity arose to take over the original boathouse again the community immediately applied itself to help raise the necessary funds and it reopened in November 1991.

Originally the race included both seagoing rafts, with many from all over Scotland competing on a three-mile course around the Craig, and fun rafts, mainly constructed by locals competing over a shorter course in the West Bay. In total about 25 rafts took part. Proceedings included an offshore display by the RNLI with the Dunbar lifeboat working with an Air-Sea Rescue helicopter, while onshore, the local lifeboat crew helped man some of the many stalls.

Over the following twenty five years or so, the raft race, which is now solely competed over a course around the West Bay, has developed into a regular annual community event. With a fancy dress theme each year, participants assemble on the West Beach alongside their ocean-going hand-crafted vessels, eagerly awaiting the off, and praying their raft makes it through the first wave.

Fun and enjoyment by spectators and participants is an important factor during the day and with support from the Community Council and donations from many generous High Street traders, the event over the years, has become an important fundraising opportunity with tens of thousands of pounds raised for both the RNLI and local charities.

In 2012 as part of the Centenary celebrations for the Edington Hospital, 'The Friends', donated a new trophy to the event for 'The Best Dressed Raft'. Other awards are presented to 'The Best Pub Raft', 'The Most Sponsored Raft' and overall winner. With stalls, live music, tombola, and children's entertainment including the Family Sand Modelling competition the afternoon has become a very welcome fixture in the summer calendar.

'In Bloom'

From small beginnings, North Berwick in Bloom, a group of volunteers which first came together in the early 1990s to provide a lift to the High Street, now looks after more than twenty permanently planted flower beds and eighty planters around the town. Since 2010, volunteers are also responsible for planting, hanging and maintaining around ninety hanging baskets in the centre of the town during the summer.

Many of the plants that are used in the planters are grown on from plugs or seeds in greenhouses, and local residents often make donations of excess seedlings or plants once they have outgrown their space. The over-winter display of violas, bellis and spring bulbs is replaced every year in June with bedding plants, mixed with centrepiece permanent planting which put on a colourful show throughout the summer months before welcoming in the autumn.

North Berwick in Bloom works very closely, not only with East Lothian Council, but also with community groups such as North Berwick Rotary, and Friends of the Law and Glen and the nursery, primary and secondary schools.

North Berwick in Bloom

Tulipa Unicum, in the Lodge.

Tulip Festival

2012

NORTH BERWICK IN BLOOM

Above Left : In spring 2012 'In Bloom' held its first Tulip Festival for which over two thousand bulbs were planted.

Below Left : Coos' Green community bed planted by local residents, using plants donated by residents of North Berwick, augmented by other plants acquired by 'In Bloom.'

Below Centre : Permanently planted bed outside Scottish Seabird Centre containing over 30 species of plants that grow on local coasts, which stand up well to salt laden winds and dry conditions.

Below Right : A few of the beautiful hanging baskets that adorn many of the High Street shops during the summer months.

North Berwick Swimming Pool

-The Last Splash

Despite a campaign by local residents to save the pool, including a petition with over 4000 signatures, North Berwick outdoor swimming pool closed for the final time at 6pm on the 26th August 1995. An aqua spectacular on the 17th August 1995 marked the end of an era in the town. Former pond-masters Eric Smith and Drew Kennedy reunited to ensure that the pool went out with a giant splash and not a trickle. Lifelong friends, both had performed throughout Britain and abroad as an acrobatic double-act 'The Cortez Brothers', in the 1950s, working with stars such as Harry Worth, Roy Castle and Larry Grayson.

Their 'Last Splash' gala, with performances at 2.30 and 7.30pm, attracted hundreds of spectators and was compered by Jack Martin, the children's entertainer. A diving display was given by the Edinburgh Diving Club, followed by an exhibition in the art of synchronized swimming and finally with Eric and Drew treating the crowd to a display of comedy diving.

THE LAST **BIG** SPLASH
at
NORTH BERWICK OUTDOOR POOL
Saturday, 26 August 1995
2-6 pm

Come along and join in the fun including:—
Treasure Hunt, Barbecue, Face Painting, Bouncy Castle and Aqua Run (weather permitting)
+
Eric and Drew Spectacular
Radio Forth Hit Squad
Lucky Dip
and much much more!!

Please note: The pool will be open for swimming as usual on 27 and 28 August 1995 from 2-6 pm

DEVISED & PRODUCED BY
ERIC SMITH & DREW KENNEDY
NORTH BERWICK OUTDOOR POOL CLOSING SPECTACULAR
17th AUGUST 1995
LAST SPLASH
PERFORMANCES 2-30pm & 7-30pm
ADULTS £2-00 CHILDREN £1-00
O.A.P & DISABLED £1-00
TICKETS AVAILABLE AT CASH DESK
RESERVED SEATS AVAILABLE
01620-892083

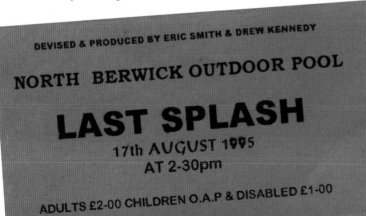

DEVISED & PRODUCED BY ERIC SMITH & DREW KENNEDY
NORTH BERWICK OUTDOOR POOL
LAST SPLASH
17th AUGUST 1995
AT 2-30pm
ADULTS £2-00 CHILDREN O.A.P & DISABLED £1-00

Centre right : Clowns awaiting their turn to join in the merriment during the 'Last Splash'.

Right : Jack Martin during rehearsals for the 'Last Splash'.

North Berwick Highland Games

The first Highland Games were held in 1996 when about 4000, mostly local, spectators attended. Today many of the attendees, who can number over 10,000, come from throughout the United Kingdom, with a fair number from overseas and many more foreign visitors competing in the various competitions held throughout the day, particularly those involving Pipe Bands.

Organisation for this annual event – health and safety and road traffic issues as well as bookings, publicity and finance to name but a few, takes up to twelve months by the small voluntary Games Committee. In addition, over the years, a considerable number of volunteers have contributed their time and effort on the day to ensure the smooth running of the event and in particular the sterling effort by members of the Rotary Club of North Berwick who give their free time to manage the traffic and parking on what has become one of the busiest days in the town's calendar.

Pipe Band competitions are held throughout the day with both juniors and seniors competing, and also a separate competition for Drum Majors. The Lothian and Borders Pipe Band Championship is also held during the Games. Visiting bands from overseas have included bands from France and Denmark and from further afield, bands representing New Zealand Police, City of Blacktown (Australia), 78th Fraser Highlanders (Canada), the Royal Army of Oman, Benoni-McTalla (South Africa) and San Diego in the USA. Bagpipe music can also be heard at its best during the solo piper competitions by the members of the Competing Pipers Association.

Other events taking place include Highland Dancing, when competitors of all ages perform the intricate steps of dances such as the Highland Fling and Sword Dance. In the Heavy Events competition competitors compete over six events, including throwing the 16lb Scots' Hammer and Tossing the Caber, with the overall winner the man who gains most points from all six events.

The day ends when all the Pipe Bands parade into the arena to salute the Chieftain of the day. After the presentation of trophies and as a stirring finale, the bands march down to the High Street to entertain the crowds there.

Clockwise from top left : Parade of past chieftains 2010; throwing the Scots hammer in the Heavy Events competition c2006; Royal Army of Oman Pipe Band marching along the High Street after the 2006 Games.

Below and previous page : Salute to the Chieftain. c2010

Scottish Seabird Centre

The concept of the Scottish Seabird Centre was created and developed by local residents in the early 1990s. The idea was to use the latest technology to allow people to see the amazing wildlife on the local islands, without disturbance. It was hoped that a custom-built Centre would help to revitalise the town's tourism, provide a new asset for locals and help to regenerate the historic harbour area.

After major community fundraising initiatives, including a "Buy a Brick" Campaign run by the Centre's wonderful group of volunteers, the Centre was opened by Prince Charles on 21 May 2000.

The award-winning Centre is a conservation and education charity that is now established as one of Scotland's top tourist attractions and a world leader in remote wildlife viewing.

After again winning the Queen's Award for Enterprise, the Queen visited the Centre on 2nd July 2009 to present the award – the first visit by a reigning monarch to the Royal Burgh of North Berwick for over 100 years. It was a wonderful day of celebration and enormous pride at what had been achieved by the many people who had supported this community-based charity and had made it such an outstanding success.

Today, the Centre continues to build on its success for the increasing benefit of wildlife, visitors and the local community.

Top Left : David Attenburgh, a popular visitor, in 2010.

Above : The Queen's visit to the Centre on 2nd July 2009 - the first monarch to visit the Royal Burgh in over 100 years.

Centre Left : The Discovery Centre, the heart of the Seabird experience, with its Wildlife Theatre, Flyaway Tunnel and Environment Zone.

Bottom Centre : Ronnie Corbett unveiling Geoffrey Dashwood's sculpture of a Tern on 30th July 2008.

Scottish
Seabird
Centre

Fringe by the Sea

Started in 2008, Fringe by the Sea is an extravaganza that has brought some of the excitement and variety of the Edinburgh Fringe down to North Berwick. The brain-child of Eric Wales and John Shaw, and with the involvement of Jane Thomson, who has considerable experience in large-scale concert promotion, the first festival was put on in August of that year. The festival took place over five days using four venues and offering 16 performances of music and comedy.

The stated aim was to quickly become the foremost 'small scale', multi-arts, non-urban Scottish festival – and by 2011 a 600 seat Spiegeltent was brought to the harbour area as the centrepiece for an event that ran over seven days in six venues, presenting some 70 paid performances to over 7,000 people. The music and comedy was augmented by theatre, film, authors in conversation, educational talks and walks, and a bespoke children's programme.

Not only was a loyal audience from East Lothian established, but the number of tourists and visitors to the town increased specifically for the period of Fringe by the Sea. In only a few years, the three organisers have managed to produce a showpiece event – celebrating arts in all its facets and mixing big names with up-and-coming young talent, bringing razzamatazz, colour and vibrancy, which has had a huge impact on the summer life of the town.

Above : Always popular at Fringe by the Sea, Scotland's most popular swing and jazz combo 'Fat Sam's Band'.

Below left : 'Orkestra del Sol' sharing their inimatable sound with a drive round the town.

FRINGE BY THE SEA
11 -16 AUGUST 2009

EDINBURGH to NORTH BERWICK
MUSIC AND MUCH, MUCH MORE
For full details and booking tickets
www.fringebythesea.com